PARIS
LETTERS

Janice MacLeod

sourcebooks

Published by Sourcebooks, Inc.
P.O. Box 4410, Naperville, Illinois 60567-4410
(630) 961-3900
Fax: (630) 961-2168
www.sourcebooks.com

Library of Congress Cataloging-in-Publication data is on file with the publisher.

Printed and bound in the United States of America.
VP 10 9

For Áine Magennis.
Thank you for introducing me to a bigger world
through your letters.
They were the seeds of my dream.

"As you move toward a dream, the dream moves toward you."

—Julia Cameron, *The Artist's Way*

Author's Note

To write this book, I relied upon my journal, my blog, and my memory. I lay it out here pretty much how it happened. Longtime readers of my blog will recognize some of the content as it was inspired by posts intrinsic to telling this story.

There are a few composite characters in this book, and some names and characteristics have been changed to protect people's privacy. One notable exception is Christophe. His name really is Christophe (Krzysztof in Polish) and to change one thing about him would be a travesty.

I omitted a few places I traveled and a few people with whom I traveled because neither had an impact on the story. Most of the men described in this book have been given more stunning qualities than they actually cultivated in themselves because that is how I once rolled. But that was before. After, naturally, came later.

We Met at a Café in Paris

I'm in love with the butcher," I told Summer. We were sitting outside Shakespeare & Company, an English bookstore on the Left Bank, just beyond the shadow of Notre Dame Cathedral in Paris.

"That was fast. I thought you were vegan?"

"I was. I am. But I'm in Paris."

Paris, it seems, was the beginning of letting go of who I was and grabbing hold of who I was to become. It was the spring of 2011. I had recently left my job and my life in Los Angeles and booked three months to traipse around Europe. Six weeks in Paris, three weeks in the United Kingdom, the rest in Italy.

"Is he in love with you too?" she asked.

"We haven't spoken." I hesitated. "But the other day when I ordered my coffee at the café across from his shop, we locked eyes. Yesterday, when I walked by, I said *Bonjour* and he said *Bonjour* back. And this morning, I said the same and he replied with *Bonjour, mademoiselle.*"

"Progress!" She laughed and slapped my shoulder like she was my oldest and dearest friend, instead of what she really was, someone I met at the airport baggage claim at Charles de Gaulle a few days before. Summer had approached me and asked if I'd ever taken the train to the city center. I said I hadn't but I was going to figure it out. She grabbed her bag off the belt and said she'd follow me. After an hour on the train, we had decided to spend a few days navigating our way around Paris together during the week she was here. Paris was a big town, and it would be nice to have someone with whom I could get my bearings.

She had a loud, raspy roughness about her that made me wince, but even the ones you don't like, you like better in Paris. When you travel, you release the usual hang-ups because you need to cling together in the face of a foreign culture. Making friends on the road is a mix of sympathy and surrender. This friend looked like she had always been on the Blond Ambition Tour. Her long blond extensions fell perfectly down her back, her big blue eyes were topped with long eyelash extensions, and her lip gloss glistened in the warm spring sunshine.

"Why don't you talk to him?" she asked as we perused *les livres* on the sales rack outside the bookstore. She wanted to buy a book and get it stamped with the bookstore's famous logo as a souvenir.

"No way. What if he speaks French back? If he said more than '*Bonjour, mademoiselle*' to me, I'd stare back with my tongue in knots." I was required to take French in elementary school and high school in Canada, but I spoke French to other English-speaking students and we only read what was in our *livre*. Here in France, they could say *anything*, and I was not prepared for *anything*.

"What does he look like?" She was flipping through a French cookbook.

My butcher boyfriend bore a striking resemblance to Daniel Craig. He had light brown hair and the blue eyes of mystics and madmen. His striped shirt was rolled up past his elbows, revealing the beginning of a tattoo. Each morning, he would lift a spit of chickens from the top of the rotisserie and lean it against the table. He slid them off one by one with a long fork, piling them in a pyramid on the warmer. He and his sexy jeans would then bend down to stir up the potatoes that were roasting in drippings at the bottom of the oven. When that was done, he would stand up, lean against the wall, look my way, and smile.

I felt steam.

"So do I," Summer said, fanning herself. "Where is this café?"

It was on rue Mouffetard, the city's oldest market street. From there, I could watch the parade of people and pooches picking up morsels from each shop along the cobblestone street. In one direction, I spotted two wine shops, two fish shops, and a fruit market. In the other direction, two bakeries, two bistros, and another fruit market. And directly across from me, a butcher shop featuring a blue-eyed James Bond.

"I can't talk to him," I said. "I could hardly even order a coffee in French."

On my first morning at the café, the waiter came by to take my order.

"*Café latte, s'il vous plaît,*" I sputtered.

"*Café crème,*" he corrected.

I nodded and blushed. This would be my first of thousands of linguistic corrections in Paris. A *café latte* is about the same as a *café crème*, but this isn't Italy or Starbucks. Steve Martin once joked that the French have a different word for everything. And here, it's not *latte*. It's *crème*.

Sitting with my *crème*, I pulled out my journal to write. It was March 2011, and I had been keeping a daily journal for the last fourteen months. But on this day, for the first time, I had nothing to write.

I looked up at the butcher. He looked over at me.

I blushed. He did not.

I picked up my pen and began:

Dear Monsieur Boucher,

I wish I could speak French.

I would ask you many questions. How did you come to stand outside la boucherie *all day selling chickens? Do your feet get tired? Your back? Your arms? How do you keep your mind occupied? How do you feel about everyone walking along and you staying in one spot? When you look down at your phone, are you looking for a text from a girl? Where do you go at the end of the day? Are you going to meet her? Has anyone ever told you that you look like Daniel Craig?*

I imagine that you follow a sports team passionately and that the friends you have are friends you've had for life. I imagine they are good people. You seem like a good person.

I watch you smile at children. You lean down to hear little old ladies. You shake hands with men. You check me out.

I wish you could sit with me here at the café. You would speak French. I would speak English. We would not understand each other, but we would grin and offer up sheepish smiles.

We could take a lifetime to piece together a conversation. It would be nice.

Bonsoir, mon ami mystérieux,
Janice

"You wrote the butcher a letter?" said Summer. We were squeezing our way through the crowded bookstore. "Did you give it to him?"

I shook my head. Instead of giving him the letter, I had tucked it into my purse, paid for my coffee, and struck out for the day.

"Give it to him. You could score two weeks of kisses along the Seine!" she said. "Isn't that what you're here for? That's why I'm here. I'd love a little French romance on my Parisian adventure."

My plan here in Paris sounded lame by comparison. I was here to take pretty photos for my blog and to warm up my language skills. Three days in, I was able to order my *crème* with my waiter and say *Bonjour* to the butcher. Progress? I sighed. "We don't even speak the same language. It would end like it always ends."

"Or not," she said.

I hadn't considered that option before. That it could not end. I thought of my letter. I didn't know at the time that the letter full of questions for the butcher would lead to a lot of answers.

Books were piled to the rafters and in messy stacks along the stairs. Some were new, most were Gently Used, according to the sticker on the bindings. Sometimes, you could even pick up an old book and discover that it had been signed by the author to George Whitman, the original owner of the store.

George found himself in Paris after World War II. He hadn't been too eager to return to America, so he enrolled at the Sorbonne University to study French. During his studies, he had amassed a rather large collection of English books. If you've ever studied language in a foreign country, you know that you *should* immerse yourself fully and turn away from your mother tongue in order to get the new language to stick in your head. But what often happens is that you become even more eager to read books in your own language, find friends of your own language, and do all you can to rest your brain from the mental pushups of learning the new language. Eventually, George had amassed so many English books that he decided to open an English bookstore. He soon expanded to digs on the bank of the Seine where it sits today, welcoming rebelling French language students and English writers for over fifty years.

Summer bought a book about the history of burlesque in Paris. I thought back to the butcher and bought a French-English dictionary.

2

How Much Money Does It Take to Quit Your Job?

Before I arrived in Paris, I was living in California, working as a copywriter in an advertising agency. I was thirty-four, single, lonely, feeling unfulfilled by my job, and on the brink of burnout. Something had to change.

I wanted to be an artist, someone who could make a great living creating something lovely. So I made a New Year's resolution in January 2010 to do just that. In Julia Cameron's book *The Artist's Way*, she details how to become an artist. One of her instructions is to write three pages a day in a journal and the answers will come. She explains that in writing, "many changes will be set in motion. Chief among them will be the triggering of synchronicity: we change and the universe furthers and expands that change." She continues with a note, which excited and frightened me in equal measure. "Leap, and the net will appear."

So I started writing in my journal. Three pages a day for a year. I also started a blog so I would be accountable to an invisible populace. We would discover together if writing three pages a day in a journal could turn me into an artist. It was a small leap, but it gave me hope that I could change my life, or at least enhance it. Really, I just wanted to create something that made me feel good, because what I was currently creating definitely did not.

I wrote junk mail. I wrote the garbage that goes straight from the mailbox to the recycling box. No flashy car commercials for me. No hip billboards. No. I wrote true junk mail. I mucked up websites with ads, stuffed bills with flyers, and inundated the public with information on products they probably didn't care about and likely never asked for. That was me. Mailing out perfect forest after perfect forest of perfectly useless messages from Fortune 500 companies. I was directly involved with the noise of daily life.

You know that letter you received from the car insurance company about how you could save big if you switched now? That was me. And the one from your phone company that told you if you upgraded to a family plan, everyone would save? That was me too. And those extra slips of advertising in your electric bill, gas bill, and credit card bill? Me, me, and me.

I'm not a fan of this legacy of garbage but, as my colleague Jeff always reminded me, the checks cleared. Copywriting gave me two things I loved: those checks and something impressive to say about my career at parties. Everyone thinks advertising is slick. But it's only slick in a greasy kind of way.

Sure, on occasion I had the chance to do a fun TV spot, but TV spots are big-budget endeavors, and with the stock market decline of 2007 followed by the flailing economy, companies were going for cheaper modes of getting the word out: direct mail.

During the first month of writing in my journal, I had a lot of questions about how I had become so miserable with my life. On the surface, everything looked fine. I was making a decent living. I had an apartment in Santa Monica with two parking spots (which is a big deal if you live in Southern California), and I had a nice handful of friends. Life should have felt great. I had just turned thirty-four and was hanging out on a rung near the top of the corporate ladder. But it started to dawn on me that my ladder was leaning against the wrong wall. How did this happen? One question swirled in my head and finally fell onto the page:

Whose dream life am I living? Because it's certainly not mine.

I scanned through the history of my decisions for clues on how I arrived at this place. Immediately, I had the unpleasant realization that I was, in fact, living my dream life, but it was a dream life I had created after I graduated university when I didn't know any better. I grew up; my dreams did not. Back then, more than anything, I had wanted to be a copywriter, and once I started working in an advertising agency, I learned I had a talent for it. I worked my way up to middle management, which afforded me middle management luxuries. I couldn't afford to buy a house, but I could afford an apartment in Santa Monica—not beachfront, but beachfront adjacent.

And yet.

After a decade, I was drained and miserable, and I knew I couldn't fulfill this dream for the long haul.

At the beginning of my advertising career, someone had mentioned that it's easy to burn out. I thought this was crazy talk. At the time, I had just started writing the inserts that went into the phone bill, which, in advertising hierarchy, was considered a step up from writing the back of cereal boxes. I thought I had hit the big time or was well on my way to writing print ads and car commercials. Maybe one day I'd get the holy grail of advertising: a Super Bowl spot. Awards, accolades, and raises poured in. Well, they didn't pour in, but there was a consistent trickle. And I loved every bit of it. But after the millionth headline and billionth copy change, I couldn't use advertising to burn through my creative juices anymore. I was on autopilot. If writing direct mail wasn't helping to get my creative energy out, I figured I'd have to burn it up in an artistic endeavor. But what? Up until then, I had dabbled in photography, jewelry making, painting, collage, guitar, and even bookbinding, but like most New Year's resolutions, my enthusiasm for these pursuits waned, and I was left once again with plenty of creative energy but no outlet.

Could I just get another job at another agency? No, that wasn't a solution. I had been in enough agencies at this point to know, as they say in Paris, same *merde*, different pile. And honestly, if I had to work in an advertising agency, the agency I was at was as good as any other. In fact, it was probably better than most, except for the staggering number of status meetings and the meager two-week vacation policy. But there were free snacks in the kitchen and as many Post-it Notes as I wanted. I should have been spending my time being grateful.

Perhaps all I really needed was another vacation. Not some grand journal-writing experiment. Not to become an artist. Or maybe what I needed was a boyfriend. More yoga. More kale. Therapy. Meditation. It was probably just because I am a Capricorn. I could blame my parents for that one. In fact, I could probably blame them for everything. Or karma. My knees. The golf balls of knots running down my back. My mouthful of mercury fillings. My sisters. My ex-boyfriends. Who else could I blame? Let's get this party started!

No, no. No. Blaming people, places, or things wasn't going to serve me on the road ahead.

By the second month of my year of journaling, I had used reams of paper to offload my gripes about work. It didn't feel like any answers were coming, as Julia Cameron had promised. And yet, in a way, they were. By the end of February, as I literally saw before my very eyes just how much I complained about my job, a question was revealed. A question that had never occurred to me before. A question that was so juicy that I immediately abandoned the pursuit of becoming an artist. A question so startlingly simple that I am still astounded that I didn't think of it before. At the end of yet another three pages of complaining about work, I sighed and wrote this question:

How much money does it take to quit your job?

I asked my colleague Akemi. We were sitting in her office picking through our salads.

"I don't know. More than I've got," she said, scrounging at the bottom of her cardboard box for bacon bits. "Plenty. Maybe a million dollars."

"It would take me forever to make a million dollars. I'm talking about buying yourself a buffer of time so you can quit your job and figure out something else to do."

We contemplated in silence for a minute, letting this question swirl. She set down her salad. "It depends on how much money you spend in a day. Multiply that by how many days you don't want to work. Save up that amount. Easy."

I set down my salad, astounded at the simplicity of this. "It's like saving up to buy yourself your own sabbatical," I said.

"Exactly."

"How much do you spend in a day?"

"I have no idea," she admitted.

"Me neither."

"Say you spend $100 a day. That includes rent, gas, food, everything. You'd have to save $36,500 to live the same way for a year without work."

"And use that year to figure out a way to buy yourself another year."

"And so on."

"And so forth."

She picked up her salad. "But what would you do with your time?" she asked. "You're a copywriter. That's who you are." Her eyes narrowed. "Is this about the vacation policy?"

"Maybe," I replied. I swallowed hard on my kale. I was the official office griper about how little vacation time we were given. A mere nonnegotiable two weeks. I griped so loudly and so often that my boss hung a giant calendar on the wall outside my office and would mark down all the approved vacation time for everyone to see and for me to stare at from my office. While I worked my way through the pile of folders that came and went in my office, a Folder Parade if you will, I could peer through the glass and watch her conduct her Vacation Policy Parade. She would walk over to the calendar with my nervous colleagues in tow, their Vacation Request Forms shaking in their hands. She'd point at the calendar, "See here, there are already two art directors out that week. We need you in the office." Dejected without a worthy comeback, they'd slink away Charlie Brown-style, cancel the plane tickets they'd already bought, take a few Tums, and come over to my office to process what just happened.

I had tissues, a loathing for the vacation policy, and a master's degree in counseling, so they knew they were in a safe place to talk. They'd vent. I'd nod in agreement. They'd vent more. I'd nod more. I'd tell them where they had gone wrong and how they could improve their strategy for next time. "See here," I'd point at their rejected Vacation Request Form. "When you wanted eight vacation days but you only accrued four? You can only pull that off with the help of a public holiday. Plus, don't think about tacking on sick days. If you do that, you won't get paid for any of them."

Their eyes would bug out, and they'd stopped crying mid-sniffle. "What?! I won't get paid?"

I would lean back in my desk. "It's happened before." I had anecdotes about others who had to cancel flights and work over Christmas, about someone being told they hadn't accrued the time off to attend a funeral (me), about honeymoons reduced or rescheduled. Entire weddings were delayed until enough vacation days had been accrued for the honeymoons.

I was a Vacation Request Coach.

I always took one of my two weeks of vacation in Canada over Christmas to visit family. It would be months before I could take another week of vacation. I had already bought my tickets for Rome the following May and gotten my Vacation Request Form approved. I was on the calendar, which meant my vacation was as good as carved in stone. I started to wonder why I had chosen a life of twenty-minute lunch breaks, time sheets, and two-week annual vacation policies.

Akemi's phone buzzed. "An email. Subject: Main Conference Room in two minutes. Don't be late! It's from you-know-who."

By the way she jumped up, I knew exactly who it was. Taking her cue, we quickly gathered our containers, tossed them in the trash, and walked to the conference room. Being late would mean being scolded by our supervisor, who would tell us that we had to buck up and pull our weight around here. Then we would slink off and doodle hateful images in the margins of our notebooks.

Spankings, office-style.

The big emergency was a surprise office birthday party for whatshisname. Always awkward. Always necessary. These office birthday parties remind me of other dumb moments in corporate daily life, such as saying "hump day" when it's Wednesday and "one more day" when it's Thursday. We ask the same dumb questions: "How was your weekend?" on Mondays and "Got big plans for the weekend?" on Fridays. We share tips for how to make the best oatmeal in the office microwave (use cold water). We send a card around the agency with an envelope for you to throw in your extra bucks for the birthday/wedding shower/baby shower/going away gift.

When would it end?

Every time I slipped a couple of bucks in an envelope, wrote a pithy comment in a card, or sat through a sad rendition of "Happy Birthday," I couldn't help but sigh inwardly and think, *This is not my life.*

After the slick birthday cake from Ralph's big-box grocery store, I returned to my office and began writing my daily three pages. Today's journal entry took an interesting turn. Instead of griping about office birthday parties, reeling through what I should or shouldn't have said to so-and-so in our disagreement about due dates or about how much I loathed filling out time sheets and permission forms, I thought about what Akemi had said and started writing money equations. This is nothing new. People everywhere are calculating their incoming and their outgoing. They are looking at the numbers and wondering how to make more, save more, buy more, pay off more, make ends meet, or how to have more money left at the end of the month rather than more month left at the end of the money.

How much money would it take to quit my job? Could I get by on spending just $100 a day in my future life…including rent, car, bills, food, everything? This number was arbitrary because I didn't know how much I currently spent in a day. All I knew was that I could afford my current life and extras like that trip I was taking to Rome and eating out. But I still had credit card debt. I was still beachfront *adjacent*.

What I liked about her $100-a-day equation was that it was easy math. I have a wall in my brain with math. If you ask me a question about an equation, I'll answer it with a blank look. But even I can multiply a number by 100. And this basic math skill was enough to keep my pencil on the paper, fooling with numbers. Say I would have a budget of $100 a day in my future life where I'm not working. If I took 2010 to save $100 a day, I'd have to save $36,500 by the end of the year. I already had some money in savings, but not much. $100 a day is not so impossible. So the preposterous, outrageous, ridiculously large, seemingly unreachable number of $36,500 became just saving or making $100 a day. A hundred bucks is something I can imagine quite easily. I can aim for $100 a day just by going to work and saying no to that group lunch or buying that sweater.

I could make this happen. I wasn't sure how, but I'd figure that out later. For now, I had to save or make $100 a day.

Sitting at my desk with the number 100 staring me in the face, I finally understood what all the journal writing was about. I didn't need to find an artistic pursuit, a hobby, or creative outlet. I needed to figure out how to save up enough to fund my own sabbatical, or even better, get out of my job. Perhaps even my career. I would create my own *Shawshank Redemption*.

I put down my pen and stared at the number. Forget finding my true art. Forget becoming an artist. I needed to become an escape artist.

DEAR <YOUR NAME INSERTED BY A COMPUTER BOT>,

Exciting news! [It doesn't matter what news it is, I'm going to make it sound exciting. This is where I tell you that there is a great offer, but it's only available for a limited time so you'd better act now.]

The first bold subhead is usually a short version of the offer I described in the first paragraph.

That's right, I'm going to say it again because I know you won't read this whole letter, you'll scan it, so I'll sound like a broken record until you call the 1-800 number or visit us online.

The second subhead is the first selling proposition. I'll tell you why we're better than the other guys.

I'll tell you why we are the biggest, fastest, clearest, safest, and best in the league. And I'll be offering it for the best price, obviously.

The third subhead will address you and those in your target.

If you're a mom, I'll discuss family packages. If you're a student, I'll tell you about our affordable high-speed Internet. If you're a senior, I'll tell you that Medicare will cover a portion of the cost and you won't need a medical exam.

The fourth subhead will tell you that you'd better act now or you'll be sorry.

I'll write about how this is a limited-time offer, which it may or may not be. Next month I'll have another offer, which will be more or less the same as this offer. "I'll add a customer testimonial here too," to add validity to the claim.

And a final sentence that will tie to the overall concept of the campaign, unless the client changes it. Then it will say, "Act now to take advantage of this incredible offer!" or something else equally uncreative.

Signed arbitrary title

John Big Shot Client Whom I've Never Met

P.S. 90 percent of the time, you'll only read your name and the postscript so I'll give the most important information here: the offer and how to get the offer. Plus I'll mention yet again that it's a limited-time offer (not).

P.P.S. The average U.S. household receives 1.5 trees' worth of junk mail each year. In 2010, there were 114,235,996 households in the U.S. That's a lot of trees.

3

Clean Out Your Underwear Drawer

My first step to Paris started in my underwear drawer.

During the slow morning commute to work the next morning, I pondered how I could save or make $100. I looked around at the people in the cars around me. All of us in our little boxed-in lives listening to music, talk radio, or an audio book, calling friends, and trying to make use of the time we were spending in the car. All just to get through the commute. All to make it bearable. All of us off to work, trying to afford our lives. How was I going to afford my future life?

Clean out your underwear drawer.

I knew this voice. Call it God, the authentic self, my imaginary friend, or the angel assigned to my case. It was the Wise Guy in my head who was constantly calm. His voice was mine, but also not mine. When my voice trembled, his was strong. When my thoughts were frantic, his were assured. In my mind's eye, he looked like Mr. Miyagi from *The Karate Kid*. An old Asian guy who said a lot with very few words. And his presence in my car that morning was so palpable that I could have reached over and tickled his knee.

I have turned to Mr. Miyagi at times for assistance with my job. When I prayed for the next headline, I prayed to him. Sometimes I would write to him in my journal, and he would write back in my journal. And sometimes, if the deadline was looming, I would make my requests out loud. "Please give me a headline!" This was often followed by "Pretty please, pretty please, pretty please." Which was often followed by "I'll do whatever it takes. Just give me the answer before the meeting." Which was sometimes followed with a quiet "Or I'll be totally screwed." And finally, after a minute of silence, the headlines began to flow.

At this point, if I didn't have my journal out, I would reach for a napkin or a receipt to write down the lines. Or a coffee-stained pack of Post-it Notes, the back of a magazine, or a paper grocery bag. I've even written headlines on the car insurance papers stored in the glove box. Seasoned copywriters will always have a good pen in the car too. One with flow, like a Uni-Ball Vision. When the ideas came, they came fast, so preparation was key.

I spent a lot of time writing at stoplights, taking dictation from Mr. Miyagi. Was it God that wrote these headlines? Was it a genie? Was it just me? No. Yes. I don't know.

On one morning, I was sitting at a light, writing a few lines on a napkin, when I looked over and saw Jon Hamm, the star of *Mad Men*, sitting in his car waiting at the light too. He was likely on his way to the studio to play the part of someone like me. In that moment, I wanted to play anyone *but* me.

I've often walked into the morning status meeting with a handful of inky Post-it Notes and handed them over stealth-style to my art director partner, the one who would later put the ideas into layouts. The project manager would ask where we were with the concepts for the next campaign. I'd confidently respond that the concepts were complete and just needed to go into layout. My partner would have looked at me bewildered, knowing that at the end of the previous day, we had had nothing. On the way back to our offices, she would look down at the Post-it Notes, which detailed the ad with headlines and layouts, and nod knowingly.

My in-car copywriting with Mr. Miyagi was part of what

made me a successful copywriter. I had *made it*. *Making it* happened after a series of awards, promotions, and bumps in pay. Once you really *made it*, you were middle management. And if you were middle management, you had to go to the 9:00 a.m. daily status meetings. The status meeting was filled with project managers, studio managers, and creative managers who had also *made it*.

Head Mistress led the status meeting. She was like a bossy babysitter. She was on task. She was on time. She was professional. I bet if she could do anything with her free time, she would go grocery shopping or organize things or boss other people around.

Sanjay, the IT guy, unabashedly played games on his phone during the status meeting. That is, when he made it to the meeting at all.

Squealing Liam was always in attendance. He and his perfect posture were always early. He always tattled on those who were late. He was the nice kid on the playground who even the nerds hated.

I was one of the leaders of the creative department, which was filled with art directors who draw the pictures for the ads and copywriters who do the writing for the ads. Together, they would come up with the idea for the ad. I was a copywriter, but officially I was an Associate Creative Director. This title meant I qualified to sit in this daily status meeting so project managers could boss me around. Because I had *made it*.

I was typically three minutes late for status meetings. It was a passive-aggressive thing. I knew this. I was aware. If I had not been required to be in the status meeting, I would probably be three minutes early for work. I would probably be a model employee. I'd probably even have perfect posture like Liam. But as it was, I walked into a full group who picked up their pens as I sat down and opened my notebook.

Trying to stay focused and not get caught doodling geraniums in the margins was the hardest part of my job in the status meeting. Usually at some point, the back of my neck would get hot and the lion inside would start pacing the cage. Rather than roar, I nodded and let them tell me what they needed me and my department to get done.

Thoreau said that the majority of men lead lives of quiet desperation. Quiet desperation. That was me in the status meeting.

⌖

Clean out your underwear drawer.

This wasn't the first being from the ethereal realm I'd felt in the passenger seat of my car. A few years ago, a colleague of mine died of a heart attack. He and I were like peas and carrots at the office. Whenever we wanted a coffee, we'd fetch it together. Lunch plans were always a matter of private consultation before public commitment. When he didn't show up to work one morning, I began learning about grief. To mask it or heal it (I am not sure which), I would imagine him hopping in my car to go grab lunch. I'd imagined it so often that I could almost see his long legs trying to fit into my small Honda Civic. Knees to the dashboard. The same jeans. Always the same jeans. And his floppy red hair in the corner of my eye. Imagining him there led to talking with him.

"I'd like to re-create the status report," his phantom self would say. "But this time, instead of Complete Budget Reports, I'd write Buy Bananas. Instead of Send Layouts to Client, I'd write Make Magic Wands."

"You'd need magic wands," I'd say, sometimes out loud. "Because magic is the only way this is going to get done."

Then we'd howl, or rather I would howl alone in my car, and I'd feel a little less horrible about never seeing my floppy-haired friend ever again.

Clean out your underwear drawer.

After Mr. Miyagi opened his big divine mouth and gave marching orders, I thought about this mysterious instruction and realized it made perfect sense. If I were to ever save up enough to quit my job, I would want to travel. And if I wanted to travel, I'd have to pack a suitcase. And if I were to pack a suitcase, I wasn't packing my tired, worn-out underwear. So why not take care of that task now instead of later, while I was still figuring out how to save or make that $100 a day.

After the traffic cleared, I drove to work and slipped into the status meeting. Instead of the usual quiet desperation, I felt excitement. I had a marching order from Mr. Miyagi. Could it be that the more I immersed myself in my pursuit to leave this job, the more insignificant it would become, and thus, less annoying?

Clean out your underwear drawer.

That evening, I went home and did just that. Turns out it takes virtually no time to sort through an underwear drawer. I didn't have to try each pair on to see if it would fit the way I did with the clothes in my closet. A quick glance at each pair made sorting easy. Many pairs were pitifully worn out, so in the trash they went. I was shocked to learn that I had underwear from many boyfriends ago. There was Five Martini Matt, Creepy Guy, Trust Fund Baby, Barista Boy, The Animator, Googly Eye Chef, Dreds, Austin (the place), Austin (the name), Web Guy (as in feet, not occupation), Travel Writer, Australian Newscaster, and Hottie But Homeless. But like any advertising campaign, the print run ended. One by one, they drifted or I drifted. Or there were questions of geography, the future, children, religion, and age—and we all had different answers for each. Yet a decade's worth of undies was still under my roof long after the lover for whom they were purchased walked out the door.

And then there were the panties to wear for Spencer. These were reasonably newer than the rest. Lacy red with a matching bra. Spencer was an architect I'd read about in a magazine. He had been a visiting professor at a local university. His tiny postage-stamp-sized portrait beside the article was just as interesting. Blond curls framed his blue-eyed, smiling face. He worked on disaster-relief and environmental projects—admirable, which made him all the hotter. His brief bio said nothing about a wife or children, but it gave me a website. I emailed him a fan letter. He responded quickly, saying that he would be visiting my city and would love to meet.

The first day of school, the first kiss, the first day at a new job…all as nerve-wracking as that moment I met Spencer. I still didn't know at this point if he was single. I just knew I wanted to know him. I met him at the university. He walked up to me with his smile. I shot back my most winning grin. He showed me the projects he was working on with his students. Afterward, we walked around campus. Cheerleaders and book-laden students in football jerseys sauntered along in jovial groups, ivy crawled up redbrick walls, and everyone wore school colors. I felt like I was on a movie set.

We found empty chairs outside a café, and he began interviewing me on my marital status, to which I responded with flirting. To which he responded with a month of late-night deliveries of Chinese food, serenades on my couch, and smooches that lasted to the early morning. But when the project was done, so was he. Off he went to the next project in the next town, likely thinking we had had a lovely time and life moved on.

I was devastated. I had believed in the story of us, from seeing him in a magazine all the way to applauding his do-gooder projects well into old age. But no. He had moved on to other do-gooder projects. A year went by with little more than a comment here and there on my Facebook page. When he did leave a comment, my day was made. He was the emblem of all the relationships that didn't work out. He got all the glory. If I could have made things work with him, I wouldn't have felt defective. He was the hero of my heartache, the knight that could have, but never did, rescue me from my loneliness.

I folded my red lacy panties and placed them back in my drawer. Soon, I had a big drawer with a tiny pile of underwear, all neatly folded like envelopes. This was more than just satisfying. A tiny chasm opened in my soul, and peace began to trickle in. I felt lighter.

Cleaning out my underwear drawer was such a lovely feeling that in the weeks that followed, I moved on to cull all my closets, except for the closet of art supplies. Too overwhelming. I opened it once and quickly shut it before a metal Prism pencil box fell on my head. Best to stick to clothes.

There were those slimming black Corporate Barbie pants. They had to stay for now. I had plenty of office meetings in my future before I could toss them. But what about the other black slacks that never fit as well or looked as good as the miracle Corporate Barbie pants? Those slacker slacks could go. As could the rest of the clothes that just didn't work on my body for one reason or another. Did I need those T-shirts that had shrunk in the dryer so I'd have to constantly tug them down over my midriff? No. And what about those sundresses that I loved so much and wore so often *five years ago* that I never wore anymore? Tossed. Or those shirts with the armpit stains that never came out. Was that deodorant or me? Those had to go.

This first swipe of my closet was a weeding out of clothes that weren't worthy to be worn in public by anyone anywhere, the ones that not even the thrift store would want. Immediately my closets looked better. And the feeling of spaciousness felt so good that I took another swipe a few weeks later. This time, I gathered all the clothes that *were* worthy to be worn in public, but no longer by me. Dresses that were just short enough to make me not want to wear them. Jeans that I never chose because I already had my favorites. And shoes. Why did I ever think I was a high-heel girl? All these B-list clothes were stuffed into garbage bags, heaved in my car, tossed with a thud at the donation drop-off door of my local thrift store, and replaced with a yellow tax write-off receipt.

Returning to my apartment after donating my clothes made me feel so great that the last thing I wanted to do was to go out and buy more clothes. In fact, it made me never want to buy anything ever again.

Did I make $100 a day cleaning out my closets? No. But it convinced me to avoid the mall, thereby keeping money in my pocket. And after feeling the weight of bag after bag heading out of my apartment, I wondered why I had bought all these clothes. Did I buy them to bring me happiness? Did they? Not really, no. In fact, they got in the way of what I was looking for.

Immediately after the great decluttering of my closets, I discovered a side effect from all that closet space. *There is a certain freedom in not having so many choices.* I knew I had less choice of what to wear, yet it didn't feel that way. Being able to keep my short inventory in my head made me feel like I had more choices. Plus, there was no more lost time in *scrounging*. And that kept me satisfied enough to not spend what little free time I had buying clothes I didn't need that didn't make me or my wallet happy.

I found this new happiness curious, so I did a little research. Unclutterer.com defines an unclutterer as "someone who decides to get rid of the distractions (clutter) that get in the way of a remarkable life." Was that happening to me? Was I getting rid of the things that got in the way of a remarkable life? Could I actually have a remarkable life underneath all this *stuff*? And could my remarkable life have started just by folding my undies into pretty little envelope shapes?

I felt a redefinition of self brewing. Instead of accepting Akemi's definition of me—*"You're a copywriter. That's who you are"*—I tried on other definitions of myself. *I am an unclutterer.*

Doesn't exactly roll off the tongue. *I am a minimalist.* Sort of. I'm minimalish.

In researching minimalists, I discovered a whole movement of people who were living simple, reasonably stress-free lives with very little in their closets. How did I miss this entire movement?

I must have been out shopping.

4

Take Care of
Unfinished Business

By the end of March 2010, three months after beginning my
year of journaling dangerously, my closets were sparse and
gorgeous. Most nights, I'd arrive home after a long day of work
at the advertising agency and be met with a mailbox full of junk,
some of which I had created during my day job. I'd briefly check
to see which headline the client had chosen before I tossed the
pile in the recycling bin.

I'd open the door, drop my bags, and then it was time. Time
to open my closet or a cupboard or stare at a shelf and set my
alarm for twenty minutes. I learned that I could get a lot accomplished inside twenty minutes. After the alarm went off, I could
stop whatever I was doing and move on with my evening. But
having that twenty minutes often got me warmed up enough
to keep going until I had a bag full of clothes, knickknacks, and
books for the donation box at the thrift store and new space in
my closet that made me gleeful. One step closer, I thought. One
step closer to one suitcase.

By April, I consulted the invisible Mr. Miyagi once again in
my car on the commute to work. "What else could I do to make
or save $100 a day?"

Take care of unfinished business.

I sat with this for a minute. What unfinished business? I had
plenty. Where would I start? Once at work, I pulled out my

journal and began writing a long list of unfinished business. Once complete, I reviewed the list and decided to start with my taxes. I had to file taxes by the end of April anyway. So if I didn't know what to do to make more money, what I *did* know was that I'd have to get my finances in order. I filed my taxes and got my grocery bag full of receipts down to one envelope of necessary, organized tax information. And I got a refund. Cha-ching!

Next was getting the rest of my finances together. I had a handful of credit cards, each with a small balance. Sometimes I didn't pay these on time and was dinged with a late payment fee. Once I paid off the small balances, I canceled the cards. I was left with the one card with the bigger balance. I was only going to take one card with me on the road anyway. Why did I have so many? I went on to close a few bank accounts. Again, why did I have a little bit of money here, there, and everywhere? And then came the coins. I found spare change in my pockets and purses, car and desk. I collected all this found money and used it to buy coffee. I was amazed at how many coffees I could buy by collecting my spare change. I also collected all my coffee cards. All those cards that promised the tenth drink free. Most of my cards had a few stamps. I compiled them all and continued my free coffee for weeks.

One morning, I woke up unable to move my neck, shoulders, or upper back. The x-ray revealed a very straight neck. I thought straight was good. Nice posture. What's the problem?

"There is supposed to be a curve," said the doctor. "Were you in a car accident recently?"

I tried to shake my head no and realized I couldn't.

"Do you work a lot on the computer?" I tried to nod. I couldn't.

"I think you got whiplash from extended computer use."

"Is that a thing?"

She nodded. "Happens all the time." She wrote out a

prescription for physical therapy. I asked her for extra days off from work. She laughed. "No, but here are some muscle relaxers that will make work feel like a circus."

Kate was my new physical therapist. She worked through the knots in my back, legs, and feet. It all helped, but when she started squeezing and scrunching the muscles around my shoulder sockets, the knots began to release their stronghold. Each week I returned for my rubdown, ready to wince through my wringing. Slowly the golf balls in my back disappeared, and I was able to move my neck again and return to my journal each day to cross off items on my list of unfinished business.

All this time with Kate made me think that I should take care of all medical appointments. When was the last time I got my eyes checked and ears cleaned? Isn't it time for my annual girly parts test?

With muscle relaxers in my bloodstream, Kate on speed dial, and a clean bill of health from a handful of medical professionals, I was feeling good about life. And my day job still didn't bother me as much because I refocused my energy on my dwindling list of unfinished business.

By night, I moved on from my closets to delve into my cupboards. I tossed dried-up nail polishes and hairbrushes. I only used one hairbrush. Why did I have six? I used up the rest of my teeth whitening gel. I gave up on and tossed the recipes I'd clipped for dishes I never made. I tossed the free CD of weird music I never listen to from that yoga class I stopped going to. The old yoga mat, the deflated yoga ball, the broken yoga straps, the expired yoga membership...tossed. Half-filled journals of half-baked ideas, the stack of phone books from the last five years, broken flowerpots that I kept with thoughts of making something crafty from them, the broken frames I meant to fix...tossed. Makeup samples, swag from film industry party gift bags, sunglasses with scratches, a home phone even though I didn't have a land line anymore, chargers for cell phones I

didn't have anymore, computer boxes for computers I didn't
have either, instruction manuals for electronics that I didn't
even remember having, the wrong-sized vacuum bags I never
returned, checkbooks for accounts I no longer had…tossed.
And loyalty cards that promised savings on everything I bought.
Tossed. I'd save more by not buying.

And through all this, I collected a little stack of half-finished
letters to my friend Áine. She and I had been writing letters
back and forth for years. We haven't lived in the same city since
we met in school. When I lived in Toronto, she lived in Japan.
When she lived in Toronto, I lived in Los Angeles. When I
lived in Toronto again, she lived in Ireland. And now that I was
living in Los Angeles again, she was back in Toronto. She is an
Irish redhead in temperament and sometimes in looks, yet she's
as sweet as sugar. On our first vacation together, when I was
meeting her in Japan, we realized that we were such compatible
travel companions that we decided to see as much of the world
as we could together. She's a master at languages, and I'm good
with the map. I'll get us to a certain restaurant, and she'll order
for us. And if some fool is trying to pull one over on us, she will
whip out crazy language skills and tell him what he can do with
himself and the horse he rode in on. She's amazing. We usually
travel to places where the mountains meet the sea.

I sat next to my garbage bag and reread the unfinished letters to her. They were all on French-themed stationery: Eiffel
Tower, cafés, poodles, wine bottles, winding streets, etc. And
all my thank-you cards were emblazed with *Merci*. Why hadn't I
realized this before? Perhaps Paris would be a nice place to visit
once I made the dough to quit my job.

I mailed off the stack of letters with a note explaining that
they were unfinished but I knew Áine would understand.

At the end of May, I hopped on a plane for my pre-approved
vacation in Rome. Áine was flying in from Toronto. We met at
the airport and skipped through the eternal city, picking up boys

and gelatos on every street corner. Two boys held our interest most of all: Sandro and Marco. Dark brown eyes, heads of curly black hair, and smiles for days, they looked like living, breathing Bernini statues. For a week, we four had tossed around colorful expressions in Italian and English and added plenty of spicy innuendo. Though Romans are great with coffee, architecture, and ruling the world for centuries, the thing that they are best at is flirting. Flirting is as ingrained in the culture as gelato and the Catholic Church. It's just how they roll. Men live for the back-and-forth witty chitchat. And yes, they live for suggestive hints about what we could do here and there. It doesn't have to be real. It just has to be fun. They are all about a good laugh. Nothing is forever. Everything is fleeting. It's all about amusement in the moment.

It was then Áine and I discovered our hidden talents for flirting. A dormant skill awakened, and we were able to keep up with the locals. Waiters became our best friends. They seemed so delighted to see us, as if we'd been there before. They kissed our hands when we arrived, and they kissed our cheeks when we left. I even had one old waiter sneak a kiss on my neck by the bathroom. One waiter asked Áine to meet him at the disco that night...and she thinks he also asked for a threesome, but something got lost in translation. She didn't take him up on either invitation.

In Rome, we were adored. And we adored being adored.

In the end, nothing ever came of any of our flirting with Sandro and Marco, except for the volleying of witty repartee and innuendo. Every word spoken was a delicious suggestive morsel. Maybe it was the water. Maybe it was the brown-eyed, beautiful men. Maybe it was the wine and our overactive imaginations. Whatever it was, this week in Italy revved me up to save up, quit my job, and travel.

We spent a day at the Vatican to get saintly again after our devilish fun in Rome. When I was a kid, my class was required to go to confession twice a year, that oh-so-pleasant task of confessing all your sins to a priest who will, after he wakes up, forgive you and instruct you to recite five Hail Marys and five Our Fathers, which will wipe the slate clean and you can resume fighting with your sisters, swearing, and lying to your parents about how much ice cream you ate. My class would traipse over to the church next to the school like a line of prisoners about to be executed—not for our sins, but because we didn't know what to say. What sins do you really have when you're eight years old? The priest would sit in the confessional, and I'd recite my list of bad things.

"Bless me Father for I have sinned. It's been six months since my last confession. Since then I've sworn, fought with my sisters, disobeyed my mother and…ummmm…uhhh…and forgive me for anythingelseIcan'tremember."

The priest, in his kindness, would absolve me of all my dreadful sins and send me off with my prayers to recite in the pew. I never really bought into all this confession business, but, like most of my Catholic upbringing, I didn't really think too long and hard about it.

When I was at the Vatican with Áine, she saw something in the distance and grabbed my arm. "Hey, the English booth is open in the Confessional. Wanna go?" I nodded, figuring a confession at the Vatican would count for more because it was *the Vatican*. I didn't have too many sins to confess. I didn't want to confess sins I knew I'd happily commit again. That was hardly asking forgiveness. But off we went anyway.

So I sat there in the confessional with the priest and began, "Bless me Father for I have sinned. It's been eight years since my last confession… Since then, I've…" Silence. "The truth is, Father, that I'm just really mad at God." I was about to begin my usual rant about how my life wasn't where I wished it was and why was God doing this to me and why couldn't I get what I wanted and what was I doing wrong and why was this

happening to me and why on earth would God do this to me???
But instead of all that, I took a deep breath and said, "I just wish
I had a really good boyfriend. I've looked for a long time, and
I'm starting to think he doesn't exist."

The priest went on to tell me all the things I didn't know I
needed to hear. He said there was a plan, and if I had what I
thought I wanted, there could be problems. He said to trust, to
assume my current circumstances were for my benefit. He said
to be grateful both for what I had and what I didn't have. If I
didn't have it, I didn't need it.

Now this sounded good in theory. But I wasn't sure. This
priest was insightful. He got right to the heart of it. This insight
surprised me. I used to think that only religions of the East
had insights. Really, as silly as that sounds, I always thought of
the Catholic Church as high on doctrine and rules and low on
insight and heart. But this priest at the Vatican? He had skills.
He continued, "And please, please, please forgive yourself for
buying into the belief that something is wrong with you. You
are not defective. You didn't do anything wrong. You don't
have to do anything more. God made you perfect." He paused
for dramatic effect. "And he kept you that way."

At the end of our conversation, I added, "Oh, and forgive me
for anythingelseIcan'tremember," just to cover my bases. He
absolved me of all my sins, advised me to do the same, and sent
me off to recite a few Hail Marys and Our Fathers. Soon after,
I skipped off for gelato with Áine and Marco. Dreamy gelato.
Dreamy Marco.

On our final day, Marco hugged me good-bye, whispering
in my ear, "*Promettimi che ritornerò.*" *Promise me you will return.* I
swooned, giggled, and nodded.

After Rome, Áine and I spent a few days on the Amalfi coast.
Whenever we met somewhere in the world, we rounded up a
couple of hardboiled eggs. We wrote our wishes on the eggs
with a black magic marker and hurled the eggs into the sea.

My wish was for a sweet life. *La dolce vita*. The results of this manifestation ritual have been mixed, but we're still working on perfecting our little tradition.

I also had a Manifestation Box back in Los Angeles. I had seen *The Secret* and was well educated on the Law of Attraction. Basically, the Law of Attraction is one of those laws of the universe. "Your thoughts become things" and "the more you think about, the more you bring about" and other pithy epitaphs are outlined in the film to further illustrate the idea that when you focus on something enough, it can come true. Magically. So I decorated a shoebox and added the ingredients that I thought would bake into a happy life. Then PRESTO, it would all happen, and I'd be amazed by the accuracy of this magic little box. This box sat center stage on my windowsill as if I thought adding sun would make my dreams grow faster. I clipped photos of happy couples and tossed them in the box along with a wad of Monopoly money. I also added photos of models that looked like me but were wearing pretty dresses and were thinner. One photo was of a sophisticated woman dressed in black walking along a street in Paris. I remember wanting so badly to be her. But that was before Rome.

When I returned from Italy, I revisited my Manifestation Box and pulled out each piece of paper, each dream, and tossed it in the trash bin, including that woman walking in Paris. After emptying the box, I chucked the box itself and was left with an empty windowsill and mixed emotions. On the one hand, I felt calm when looking at an empty windowsill. I felt the same peace I had felt the day I cleaned out my underwear drawer. I also felt a pang of disappointment that my manifestation experiment didn't seem to work. But after that slight pang wore off, I turned away from the windowsill and felt a sense of relief. No more pressure to MANIFEST. As if life was one big checklist of accomplishments. I had a big enough list of unfinished business, thank you very much. I walked away from it all, not as part of a happy couple in a dress two sizes smaller, walking hand in hand in Paris. I walked away free of all that. I walked away happy to stop aiming for it. If you want to hold water in the palm of your hand, you can't grasp at it. I was willing to be satisfied with the notion that if I hadn't accomplished what was in the box, I had at least accomplished something. I had a clean windowsill.

By June, the sixth month into my journaling year, I had crossed plenty off my list of unfinished business and let go of many items, such as most of my books and one of my guitars. I was ruthless. I knew, without knowing where I was going, that I wouldn't need this stuff when I got there.

But one item stopped me in my tracks.

My Kris Kristofferson album.

I haven't owned a record player since my single-digit years, but I couldn't bring myself to get rid of this album. This record was pilfered from my parents' collection. When I was a kid, I would gawk at this album cover and stare into his steely blue eyes. Kris Kristofferson was a real artist. A great lyricist and pretty good actor. When I looked at Kris, I thought, "This guy is so good at everything he does. And what he does is so *cool*. I want to do something cool." I kept the album.

Though I didn't realize it at the time, that album was my Manifestation Box.

5

Cut Down on Groceries

By July, my slight changes in behavior were making a surprisingly big impact on my bank balance. I wasn't necessarily saving $100 a day, but I stopped buying décor items for my home and clothes for my wardrobe. I was still delighting in my sparse closet. Each month, I deposited my checks and tried to leave them alone.

This constant monitoring of money made me extra vigilant when invitations came my way. I started saying no to group dinners that included Chuggalug Chad, who always drank seven glasses of wine to my one glass and then suggested we split the bill. No, thanks, I'd rather use that extra cash to buy my own drinks, preferably at a café on a terrace while watching the sunrise over the Vatican and without you slurping and slurring next to me.

And then came the vegan thing. I never really thought much about veganism or vegetarianism beyond my mother and aunts huffing at having to make a vegetarian lasagna because a few of my veggie cousins were coming by for dinner. Then after the dinner, when everyone had left, someone would wonder aloud if vegetarianism was a healthy choice. How can you feed your children on a vegetarian diet, for heaven's sake? How can you possibly feel *satisfied* without a decent piece of meat?

That's just it. Films and books were coming out about factory farming, and I became aghast at how there are hardly any decent pieces of meat left. Factory farming made up 99 percent of the meat in our grocery stores. To find that 1 percent of meat that came from animals that had a good life and a humane death was so difficult that I threw up my hands. *The Kind Diet* by Alicia Silverstone provided me with all the logic I needed to become vegan. I want to be healthy. I want to be kind to the planet. And I could do them both just by not eating meat? I bought into the kindness factor. Sign me up.

Turns out saving the planet didn't cost near as much as ruining it. After deciding to go the veggie route, I saw I could save a lot of money, which was appealing if I were to ever quit my job and hit the road. Without the dairy and meat in my diet, my grocery bill was halved. Did I mourn the loss of burgers? Nah.

Did I mourn the loss of cheese? You betcha.

Great big sobbing mourning about not getting to have melted cheese slathered all over and oozing out of everything. Science has proven that cheese is actually addictive. The primary protein in milk is casein, which gives that satisfied reverie we cheesists feel on a soul level. I was a happy cheese addict. But I knew if I took out the meat from my diet, I'd overdo the cheese. I know me. I know what I'm capable of. My path to veganism had to be paved with oatmeal.

I thought veganism would be hard when I went out to eat. Not so. I discovered that in California, all restaurants must have at least one vegetarian meal on the menu. I started appreciating the limited options. I remembered what I learned from clearing out my closets: *There is a certain freedom in not having so many choices.*

And my body didn't seem to mind one way or another if it had meat. I was already tired and miserable all the time. I was still pretty much tired and miserable as a vegan, except now I had a glimmer of hope that it could actually be possible to save enough money to buy myself a year or two of freedom from my advertising job. And that little nugget of hope was more delicious than a chicken nugget any day of the week.

But my vegan days were over the day I sat across from the butcher shop in Paris. I'd need a reason to go in. And in Paris, they didn't have vegetarian options at the butcher shop.

6

Find an Accomplice

You don't have to worry about keeping your dreams a secret when you tell people you're going to quit your job, because they don't believe you anyway. I had mentioned this to a circle of friends at a garden party back in Santa Monica. Most nodded in that way you nod when you're not really listening. But not my friend Ben.

"What?!" he said.

"Yes," I said. "I'm thinking of starting in Europe."

He pursed his lips and crossed his arms.

Later, when I came out of the bathroom, he was standing there waiting for me. "Listen," he stammered. "I want to go to Europe. On tour. With my music."

"You want to be a rock star?"

He nodded.

"That's crazy."

"I know." He smiled. "You want to quit your job to travel and just hang out. That's crazy."

I smiled. "I know." And with that I found an accomplice.

He wasn't my first choice, I admit, but after one strange day in the car with my coworkers, I knew I had made the right choice.

On that day, I grabbed a rare lunch with a few colleagues. We piled into Akemi's Prius and headed for Indian food. That's when I announced that I had paid off my credit cards.

I had that one credit card that demanded my attention every month. It wasn't a huge amount, but I rarely paid it off so it slowly grew until it gave me a feeling of dread when I saw it lurking between the pieces of junk mail in my mailbox. But with my extra cash from saving up and selling off, I did what any good reader of Suze Orman would do: I paid it off.

If you only accomplish one thing in a year, let it be paying something off. A student loan, a car, a credit card, your bookie, whatever. The relief that follows feels like the releasing of a knot in your stomach.

Until you tell someone.

"That's great," said one coworker.

"Wow, good for you," said another.

"Are you kidding me?" said Akemi.

"I am not kidding you. I am officially debt free for the first time in forever. No student loan, no car payment, no credit card payment."

"You're, like, rich."

I laugh. "Not exactly, but it sure feels that way."

Then silence. Strange silence. The kind of silence that happens when you tell an off-color joke. The kind of silence that hangs heavy in the air. The kind of silence that's just plain weird. According to the Federal Reserve, the average credit card debt per household is $15,800. I wondered about the debt balances of my car compadres.

In Dr. Phil McGraw's book *Life Strategies*, he writes that to achieve your goal, "find someone in your circle of family or friends to whom you can be accountable. Make periodic reports on your progress." The credit card progress report hadn't worked on my lunch mates, but perhaps I could make Ben my accountability partner.

I had met Ben at a birthday party six years prior. We discovered in each other that we could both remember obscure lyrics from songs as far back as thirty years before we were born. My lyric education stems from my father's insistence on listening to the country music radio station when he was in the kitchen where the radio sat on the windowsill, my mother's insistence on gospel when she was in the kitchen, and rock when my sisters were in the kitchen. When everyone was in the kitchen, it was too chaotic so I sat in front of the TV. I was no Mark McGrath, but I could hold my own with lyrics. So could Ben. He was a songwriter at a record company by day, and occasionally he performed at bars around town.

During September, I spent long evenings at the coffee shop on Wilshire and Third Street in Santa Monica working my way through unread books from my bookshelf. One evening, I was reading at a barstool along the window and heard a knock on the glass. I looked up and it was Ben. I smiled and waved. He came in and sat down.

We looked at each other, saying nothing for a minute. He spoke first. "Why are you leaving Los Angeles?"

"I can't do this town. Somehow, my dream came true and it sucks."

"Yep."

"Yep."

And that was that. We talked out our plans for our escape to Europe with the only other person who believed it was possible. For many evenings over the next few months, I'd be sitting in that coffee shop reading or writing and he would walk by, see me, stop in, and we'd talk. We would go over lyrics he was finessing and household items I was selling. I told him I didn't know where to go once I got up the nerve to quit my job. Europe, yes, for a vacation. Then what? Just stay? He didn't know how to bridge the gap between writing songs for others and becoming a performer himself.

I started to feel stirrings for him, but by now I was already mentally packing my bags. This was no time to start anything. No illicit plans were made, no flirting, no innuendo. On one of our coffee nights, I started to pack up to go. "It's late," I yawned. "I'm heading home."

As I got up to leave, he grabbed my arm and gave me a wink. "The night is young. Let's get a beer."

And that's when I knew it. Inside this tiny, innocent moment, I knew that any stirrings would have to simmer down.

"Ben, I'm the *Early Show*."

He cocked his head, sat with this for a moment, and nodded. "I'm *Late Night*."

Understood. It would never work.

We still met at that coffee shop for many nights until I left for Europe. At times, when we ran out of ideas and suggestions, we would allow silence to hover in the air between us. Perhaps we were waiting for a voice from somewhere beyond to just tell us what to do.

7

Turn What You've Got into Something You Can Sell

I finally got around to cleaning out my art supply closet. The final mess. The closet full of unmet expectations. I pulled out all my unfinished canvases and started painting. Each night for weeks, I went straight home after work and tinkered away. I learned to quietly decline invitations when others asked me to do things. Turning people down was never my strength, but I just felt like painting more than I felt like doing anything else.

Before, I thought I needed to know what I wanted to paint before I picked up my paintbrush, but when the goal changed from painting something wonderful to painting something just to use up the supplies and finish a canvas, I managed to create some art. Inspiration, it seemed, was not required.

I knew I couldn't take these paintings on the road with me, so I opened a shop on Etsy, the online marketplace where you can sell handmade and vintage products. Setting up my account was easy. Linking it to my PayPal account was just as easy. And selling actually happened. On the site is a blog called Quit Your Day Job. It's filled with success stories of those who worked in cubicle land like me until they started making art and selling it on Etsy. Eventually they were able to quit their jobs and sell online full time.

I kept painting.

I painted a lot of crows. I didn't know at the time why; I just liked their silhouette and the fact that they excel at survival in urban environments while other species go extinct. Perhaps there was a symbolic meaning of people pecking at me all the time, always requiring something from me and me not having strong enough boundaries. Or perhaps it was simply that the table where I painted was next to the window where I watched crows squawk from the power lines. In one painting, a crow was flying above the waves of a stormy sea, struggling against the wind and waves. If he only knew that he could make flight easier if he just rose above it all.

I sold most of my paintings to friends and on Etsy. I also donated them to charity auctions and gave them as gifts. Eventually, I put the rest of my art supplies in a box and sold it too, to a mom of three who would put a big box of half used paint to very good use. As she walked off with the box, I slipped the $50 bill in my pocket and wondered if it would be traded in for dinner along the Mediterranean or a train ticket to a village in the middle of vineyards.

By November, I had reached and surpassed my goal by doing a hundred little things to save or earn $100 a day. I managed to save almost $60,000, nearly twice what I thought I'd save. Selling, saving, and being vigilant with my bank balance was just the beginning. I suggested free activities like hikes and card games with friends before they had a chance to ask me out for a pricey dinner. No one took me up on cards but hiking worked. (Burning calories always works in California.) Plus, I was already ratcheting down on friendships from the outer circle of my social sphere. I knew I would be leaving Los Angeles. It would make slipping out the back door easier.

The big boosts to my bank account came from two directions. First, the bonuses at work were double that of the previous year, the benefit of doing this project during the recession recovery. Second, I started playing the stock market after asking a few old men at my coffee shop how to begin. I learned that old men love to talk about money and are happy to share their knowledge with doe-eyed young girls. Apparently, it takes virtually no effort to open an online account and start trading stocks. I kept trading and researching, buying and selling. When I bought a stock and it went up, I sold it. If it went down, I waited until it went back to the asking price or went green. Then I sold it. Sometimes I'd make just $30. Sometimes I'd make more. I reinvested the original sum, adding a little more each time. I kept rolling the dice and praying. I also kept investing the cash from things I had sold on eBay, Craigslist, and Etsy. It felt like free money, so if I lost, I didn't freak out. I kept investing, shaving off the green, and depositing it into my swelling account. Over time, the balance grew. Perhaps it was beginner's luck. Perhaps it was just a good day at the slots. Either way, it boosted my account to the point where I had reached my financial goal. I had saved up enough cash to buy myself a buffer of time to spend it any way I like.

And that's when Spencer called to let me know just how I could spend that time.

He started by telling me that he'd seen some of my paintings online. He said he'd love to do a trade for one of his sketches. Of course, this was all just a pretense for what he really wanted to know. "I've been reading your blog, Janice," he started. "You're cleaning out your apartment and saving up cash. I need to know your plans."

I didn't add the master plan to the blog, that I would quit my job after reaching my goals. I knew coworkers and my mother read my blog. No need to cause alarm. I told Spencer that I didn't have much of a plan, though I'd like to get my life down to one suitcase and take off for Europe.

He believed me.

"Listen," he started. "I have a project. It's global. I plan on touring universities to teach about sustainability and disaster-relief projects. I'm looking for a travel companion. Do you want to come with me?"

Me? The man I adored for no good reason, the man for whom I had bought those sexy red undies, wanted to travel around the globe with me? ME! Up until that moment in time, except for my first ride on a major roller coaster when I was eight, I had never been happier.

The trouble was that he needed money. He was trying to score funding from some philanthropists. Maybe we could find something for me to do. *I've got a few ideas on what I could do, hot stuff. On what we could do together. Like fall in love, have babies, and stick them in our backpacks as we travel the world and smile at their cute, fat, dangling legs. We'd live off the land, eating organic things and changing the world. Oh sweet, wonderful, torn world, here we come to fix you!*

But he had to get the funding first so I shouldn't do anything dramatic like quit my job or anything. Or plan our entire life together in my imagination before we even hung up.

"I just need to get funding. I should know by the end of December, and we'd leave in January. Could you be ready?"

"I can leave any time." When we hung up, I looked around my spacious apartment and thanked my lucky stars that I had already cleared most of it out.

8

Write Your Resignation Letter

In December, after a string of very good days on the stock market and very bad days at the office, I handed in the resignation letter I had written a few months before. My supervisor wanted me to stay on for three weeks rather than the customary two. Triggered, I suggested one week as I had spent the last four years staying late and skipping lunch breaks. This triggered her, and we proceeded to partake in the ugliest yelling match of my career. Looking back, I could have done better. She could have done better. We could have done better.

Two weeks later (minus two days out of spite), I cleared out my office. It took about two minutes. I had been emptying the drawers over time so that my office was like a movie set. Papers were on the desk, but no files were stored in the cabinets. All that was left were folders for someone else to deal with. I closed my computer, handed in my security pass at the front desk, and left with a small box of samples of my advertising work and the apple pin I had received from Leo Burnett Advertising, my first advertising agency. When I arrived home, I emptied the box on the floor, looked at it, and laughed. There was no way I would be taking my samples with me on the road. I repacked the box and walked it out to the trash. I kept the apple pin.

Everyone who worked at my Leo Burnett office got an apple

pin. We all wore it. It was a pretty cool pin that represented membership in a pretty cool club.

Why the apple? When Leo Burnett created his advertising agency during the Great Depression, he had a bowl of apples in his lobby for employees and visitors. Naysayers said that opening an advertising agency in the middle of the Depression was a bad idea. They said he would soon be selling those apples on the street.

Today, Leo Burnett is the tenth largest advertising agency in the world, and every Leo Burnett office in the world offers apples at reception. Employees, clients, the FedEx guy, the UPS guy, everyone can grab an apple on their way in or out of the office.

I ate a lot of apples when I worked at Leo Burnett. And I really loved being a copywriter. I wore my apple pin with pride.

Since my first apple at Leo Burnett, I had done a lot of copywriting. A dozen years, thousands of campaigns, millions of words. But somewhere along the line, in all the agencies I worked at since, something had changed. They became More More More factories. More ads, more versions, more emails, more mail. More, more, more with less budget and less time.

And without adequate recovery time between churning out these ads, my work/life balance went severely off kilter. Monday through Friday became a flurry of work. Saturday became a recovery day. Sunday became the weekend. Year after year of this... Well, that's no way to live. Not for me.

Other people could do the long intense hours required of an advertising agency. They even liked it. I was just not one of these people. I was not even from the same planet as these people.

I was the crow that didn't know how to rise above the storm.

So now, I would travel the world and write about it. And I would take nothing with me from my former copywriting life except for one thing: my Leo Burnett pin. It would remind me to be grateful for what my career gave me for my journey: the friends I had made, the writing skills I had developed, and the checks that always cleared. I was grateful. But I was done.

I was also technically done with my New Year's resolution. I had written in my journal nearly every day for the year, but by now, writing was a habit and a great way for me to carve out time for myself each day to hatch my evil plans, so I decided to keep journaling. It proved to be an excellent container where I could figure things out.

I was about to start traveling. In January, I would be leaving with Spencer, who I was referring to in my head as Love of My Life. *Note to self: don't do this.*

All through December, he and I talked on the phone, excited about the prospect of hitting the road together in 2011. We imagined where we would go, what we would see. And beyond that, I imagined what might happen when our eyes were closed.

I had printed out a map of Europe and glued it into the front cover of my journal. All those squiggly boundary lines. All those countries. All those places to see. All those people to meet. All the photos I could take and the fun blog posts I could write. I had grown tired of my straight line: building the résumé, the account balance, saving for a down payment, etc. I wanted to flit about with a complete disregard for sensible living. Each day, I would trace the curvy boundary lines of my map with my finger and wonder about what the curvy route of my own line would take. Ohhh, it made my teeth tingle. And all that without a plan of where and how long?

Where should I begin? I had Spencer to figure that out. I thought so anyway. I would just wait for his call. This, of course, was our pattern. Me waiting for him to call, to arrive, to make plans, to call again because he was running late, to call and cancel. Waiting, always waiting for Spencer. Never knowing what he was thinking. Never asking. But I was willing to wait this time because I thought the romance might rekindle, plus I was scared to head out on the road alone. It would be easier to follow him around.

Two weeks of silence went by before he finally called to tell me he didn't get the funding and the trip wasn't going to happen. The call was short, somewhat sullen, and peppered with "That's how it goes" and "We must be destined for something else." I kept the tone of my voice upbeat, but I was devastated. Before he hung up, he said his customary farewell, "Aloha."

I hung up. The prospect of leaving to travel on my own became suddenly scary. I'd have to make all the decisions now. Where to go, where to stay, how to get from here to there… everything. Before, I had imagined following Spencer around like a little puppy dog. Letting him take care of everything while I stood by. Like a little wife. And now that fantasy was done too. All of it was done. Traveling with someone. A future with him. Done, done, done.

I looked around my apartment. This spacious, bright, calm place. I was so preoccupied with leaving that I hadn't spent much time enjoying the space. I realized in this moment that I could stay here. I could stay here in this apartment. In the middle of this, the phone, still in my hand, rang again. This time it was my friend Mary.

"Janice, you quit!" She had read my blog, which had had a steep increase in readership since announcing my departure from corporate life.

"Yes, I did."

"Great. Want to come to Hawaii with me? We leave in three days."

"Aloha."

9

Or Should I Say Bonjour?

Tanned and relaxed, I tipped the beach sand out of my suitcase, repacked, sold off the rest of my furniture, handed in my apartment keys, and boarded a plane bound for Paris. Why not Rome? Because I wanted to end up in Rome, not begin there. So I would start in Paris, loop up to the United Kingdom where I would meet up with friends and family along the way who were also traveling, down to Italy and…stay? Was that the plan? Was that crazy? Maybe. So was leaving my job during, and I quote Suze Orman, "the big money-making years."

I paid for my furnished flat for the six weeks I would be in Paris. The utilities were included so I had no bills. To not have bills felt like an anchor had been lifted and I was free to explore the world untethered to any responsibilities. I was free to roam.

And roam I did. In my first week in Paris, I visited the big tourist attractions with Summer: the Eiffel Tower, Sacré-Coeur, Arc de Triomphe. It was great fun, but she and I had spent the week telling the stories of who we were and what brought us to Paris. All of that was fine and lovely, but when I was finally alone, I had to admit the silence was nice.

Each morning, I sauntered over to the café to write in my journal and take in the view of my sexy butcher. If I was lucky, he would take his break while I was sitting at the café. Though he didn't approach me, he did his fair share of staring and smiling.

He would lean against the wall just beyond the butcher shop and smoke a cigarette. In my LA life, cigarette smoking was a big red flag. But here, it was just sexy. And I learned that I was in the minority as a nonsmoker. The butcher's arms were crossed over his chest as he leaned against the wall. He lifted his cigarette to his mouth, inhaled deeply, and exhaled a long cloud of smoke as he stared off at a distant thought. He would take a sideways glance at me, and I would look down to my journal. My cheeks would get warm. I would look up, and he would still be watching me. I smiled; he smiled. I exhaled. He took another drag.

Once my writing was done, I would pay for my *café crème*. By my second week, it was still too creamy for my liking, but I wasn't sure how to ask for less cream. I only knew how to ask for a *café crème* so that's what I got.

I would send my butcher boyfriend a small wave. I could feel his eyes on my back as I left. I walked slowly up rue Mouffetard toward one of the eighteen arrondissements to explore. I got lost. I would find a Métro station and look at the map at the entrance. Each map has a big *Vous êtes ici* red dot. *You are here.* Yes, but why?

I thought when I first arrived in Paris that my biggest anxiety would be the language, but that fear fell away the moment I had to use the Métro. There are 303 stations, which makes the newcomer to Paris want to walk. But I soon learned that Paris was too much city for my aching feet. Plus, the Art Nouveau design of the stations was seductive. Their curving iron tendrils drew me in, and soon I was swallowed into the belly of the city. To my surprise, delight, and relief, the Métro was easier to master than I thought it would be. Each line is color-coded and numbered, and the direction each train is going is named after the final station. And maps are everywhere—above ground, below ground, and above each door on each train. As I sat on the train, I liked to imagine those who carved out the city—likely blowing out ancient Roman ruins and catacombs in the process. No one seemed to mind though. We sat on the train in silent contemplation as we zipped under the city, occasionally verifying with a sideways glance at the map that we were, in fact, headed in the right direction.

On the morning after Summer had left, I meandered up the Seine toward one of the Métro stations, but the river was sparkling like diamonds in the morning sun so I changed directions and walked along it instead. It was a beautiful time in my life when I was alone and could change course on a whim. No one to consult. No one expecting me to be somewhere. No one to convince. Along my walk, I took in the ornate iron balconies and steeply pitched roofs studded with oval dormer windows held in place by stone angels. I crossed a bridge and arrived at Notre Dame. The windswept esplanade in front of the cathedral was always crowded with tourists, pigeons, and beggars. Gargoyles peered down to ward off evil spirits (and also served as spouts to keep rainwater from running down walls and eroding mortar: gargoyle-gargle) and the front façade was lined with carvings of saints that seem to say, "Come on in, good lookin'." So that's what I did.

Mass was starting as I walked into the cathedral, so I took a seat. My feet needed the rest anyway. As I sat, I remembered a time when I had fantasized about all the things I'd do once I arrived in Paris, such as going to mass at Notre Dame. Now here I was, wandering without a plan, and boom!

Sometimes dreams come at us sideways.

Catholic masses are the same all around the world. The priests all say the same thing in the same way: even the cadence at which they speak is the same. You may not realize it until you go to other churches in different languages, but it's easy to follow along. And since I rarely listened even in the English masses, I felt quite at home zoning out with the French.

For me, the church had always been quiet and uneventful,

and that's how I liked it. When I was a kid, I sat next to my sisters, mom, and grandma. Cousins and classmates filled the surrounding pews. I'd respond to the responsorial psalms and stand, sit, and kneel along with the congregation, but my mind was wandering or blank. Or I would stare at how the sun glimmered through stained-glass windows, making kaleidoscope patterns on the bald heads of those in front of me. The stained-glass scenes depicted were those of Jesus's greatest hits: the miracles, healing the sick, the walk up Calvary Hill, the crucifixion, the rising from the dead. And then there were the rows and rows of saints that peered down from above with their arms raised to either give a blessing or wave. (Hey, good lookin'!)

The Catholic Church offers a slew of saints that you can pray to for every issue in your life. Saint Anthony is one of my favorites as he is the patron saint of lost things, and since I was traveling with only the essentials, I was paranoid about losing any of them. He's even got his own rhyming prayer: *Dear Saint Anthony, please come around. I've lost my (fill in the blank), and it cannot be found.* My sister once said of Saint Anthony, "Watch what you ask for from Saint Anthony. It really works. You've got be careful. You've got to really want it back."

There is Archangel Michael, who will cut your ties with whatever and whoever you want out of your life. And then there is Saint Christopher, who I thought of a lot as he is the patron saint of safe travels and that's exactly what I was praying for. The greatest daily threat to a traveler's life is traffic. After a few close calls with scooters, I had rubbed the Saint Christopher medallion around my neck more than once in thanks and prayer. Notre Dame has its own special saint. Apparently, Saint Louis IX was the King of France and he bought the Crown of Thorns from Baldwin II of Constantinople. I wonder if he prayed to Saint Anthony to help find it.

After I had peeled the bland Eucharist off the roof of my mouth and Quasimodo rang out the last bells of mass, I joined the procession out the door and headed down the river to Saint-Germain-des-Prés in the 6e arrondissement to find myself a crêpe. It was a chilly day in March, and I was looking for something warm and toasty. Now that I didn't have a steady income, street food occasionally served as the big meal of the day. I walked down a market street lined with restaurants and tourist shops and found a crêpe stand where they whipped up a crêpe with egg, mushroom, and cheese.

With my first bite, I almost fell over. The paper-thin warm pancake enclosed the cheese, which pulled the egg and mushroom together in a trinity of amazing.

One word: Eucharist.

How had I ever been vegan?

10

Gustav Who?

Everyone thinks they'll see the Eiffel Tower from everywhere in Paris, but she's rather elusive. The apartment-lined streets often hide her from view until you turn the corner onto a grand boulevard. Suddenly there she is, gazing down at you in all her lacy steel glory.

I had been walking for an hour and not yet laid eyes on her. The day was cloudy, and the wet mist seeped through my coat and scarf. I was sure I was heading straight for her, but there are no right angles in Paris, only a maze of triangles. I was hoping the sun would come out and I could have a picnic on the grass in the shadow of the Eiffel Tower, but my stomach was rumbling and my feet were aching, so I sat in the park next to the Rodin Museum to eat lunch and review my map. I unwrapped my baguette, which was sliced and buttered. Never in my life in Los Angeles would I have indulged in this carb and fat feast, but in Paris, it felt right. Plus, I still ran my calories consumed vs. calories burned calculator in my head, a niggling habit I retained from my former California life. They say the farther you walk, the smaller you get. I was walking enough.

Each time I ate bread during that first month in Paris, my grandmother came to mind. For long summers of my childhood, I sat at her kitchen table waiting for her to slice the warm bread fresh from the oven. Her slices were always thick and slathered with butter that melted on contact. The crisp crust gave way to a soft and chewy center. This was the kind of bread you never put in a toaster, not that it would fit. This bread was too special for toasting. This bread should be eaten warm and not dressed with anything but butter. With this bread, I felt fed from my head down to my toes that dangled from my chair.

I looked down at my baguette. *The French eat this every single day!* They know the feeling of being fed by bread in a way that I hadn't felt fed since those summer days at my grandma's kitchen table. The sun came out and burned off the mist. I looked up, and there was the tower in the distance. Oh right, you!

The world's most recognized monument was built as the entrance to the world's fair of 1889. Located on the Left Bank of the Seine, it has become the icon and main attraction of Paris. But it was never meant to be a permanent structure. The plan was to disassemble the tower after the fair, but by then radio towers were popping up in major cities, and it, being the tallest structure, remained in place as a beacon for emitting and receiving radio signals. The tower itself is a remarkable example of architecture.

When Gustav Eiffel started building, he noticed two of the four leg foundations would have to be built below the water level of the Seine. To avoid creating the leaning tower of Paris, he dug deep and poured massive foundations. Good thing he was a bridge builder. If you look at the Eiffel Tower with your head cocked to one side, it's easy to imagine it as one half of a bridge. At the time, the tower had many critics. They called it vulgar, a great phallus in the sky. But Gustav Eiffel was steadfast in his reasoning behind the design. Mathematics dictated the shape: the stress of the structure equals that of the wind from any direction. And the lattice lets that wind pass right on through. Strong elegance. Nice.

When I learned how the tower was built, I saw Gustav Eiffel less as an architect and more as an artist. He took the elements of water and air, added the materials he had to work with, and created a structure that couldn't possibly have worked any other way for what they knew of tall structures at the time.

Lunch eaten and feet rested, I continued toward the Eiffel Tower. Upon approach, the mood definitely changed. Tall African men stood and jangled large rings strung with mini replicas of the Eiffel Tower. "One euro, one euro." Gypsies begged for money. "One euro, one euro." And the thieves started appearing. The worst of all the pickpockets were the survey takers. Young girls and boys walked around the major tourist areas with clipboards and pens. Here is how it worked: They came up to you and asked you to sign a petition. You, being the kindhearted tourist you were, who was also slightly confused by this stranger standing so close, looked down at her clipboard with a fake survey attached. While you were reading this fake petition that saves Who Knows from Who Cares, they were slipping their hands into your pockets to swipe your phone, wallet, and whatever else they could grab. If the girl with the survey wasn't picking your pocket, her friend who snuck up behind you was quietly relieving you of the spare change and Métro tickets in your backpack.

I had seen them around and was warned about them repeatedly. These thieves triggered me like no other, partly because they were so good at picking pockets and partly because they hounded. When one was done hounding, another came along a minute later. Soon the dreamy Eiffel Tower experience turned into me clutching my purse and yelling. They wouldn't take a polite no for an answer. Only an aggressive "*Non!*" along with finger pointing followed by "I'm not a tourist, you thief!" yelled in French. I would have followed up with swear words, but I didn't know any in French and wouldn't know where to fit them into a sentence anyway.

If anyone ever got too close to me, which was a natural tendency in crowded places in front of monuments, and if they tried to get their hand in my pockets, they would have to get their sneaky hands past my tissues barricade. I had a layer of crumbled tissues, some used and some not, on the inside of my bag. My tactic was to gross them out. I reasoned that touching a damp tissue would deter them from going any further.

Then there was the ring trick. A young boy would walk by me and pretend to have picked up a ring next to me. He would ask if it was mine. I would tell him it wasn't. He would offer it to me. If I accepted it, he would ask me to give him money for it. Luckily, I knew about the non-finger-pointing strategy before my ring bearers came along. "*Non!* I'm not a tourist, you thief!"

And there was the long-winded tales of woe trick. This one I actually fell for. A man stopped me on the street and asked for two euros to buy an inhaler, pleading on my Good Samaritan nature. Naturally, he had lost his wallet. Naturally, he was having a hard time breathing. Only when I opened my wallet and his face turned ever so slightly from a look of desperation to a look of glee did I know I had been had.

Eventually, I could spot them coming. I saw girls walking out of malls with too many handbags, running over to the man roasting chestnuts and stashing the loot in the boxes behind him. *The chestnut roaster is in on it!* The girls would continue on, lurking around unsuspecting tourists to snatch more handbags. Once I came upon a middle-aged American couple trying to read a survey from one of the quick-fingered heathen survey-takers. The couple was quietly being swarmed by pickpockets. Something came over me, and I went berserk. Clutching my own bag with one arm, my other arm flailing, I ran up and started yelling like an angry pigeon. "Thieves! *Voleurs!* Pickpockets! It's a scam! They are trying to steal your money!" The thieves scattered, not wanting to make a scene so they could quickly get to the next set of tourists. When they left, I stopped flailing and kept walking, yelling back,

"Have a nice vacation!" The middle-aged American couple looked baffled by the whole scene.

Besides all the thieves, standing at the base of the Eiffel Tower and looking up was still breathtaking. Taking the elevator to the top and peering down at the rooftops of Paris was still marvelous. The only problem was that when I was standing at the top, the skyline of Paris didn't look quite as it should. It was missing one element: the tower itself.

Back on solid ground, I continued walking. This time I was on a mission to Le Bon Marché, one of Paris's major department stores. The highlight here wasn't the luxury purses or even the building itself, which was also designed by Gustav Eiffel. It was the food section. Since arriving in Paris, I had an insatiable appetite. Was it because I was walking so much or was it simply because I had deprived myself so often for so long?

Walking into the store, I came upon the fish section. Glistening oysters lounging on platters of crushed ice and fish gawked with their stunned, staring eyes. I continued to the chocolate section and gasped at the gravity-defying sculptures. I stood mesmerized by rainbow walls of fruity *confitures* and marveled at vibrant shelves of canned sardines, mussels, and paté. I was mystified by round mounds of cheese ranging in shades from creamy brie and ashen chèvre to speckled blue Roquefort. At the pastry area, I became befuddled, trying to decide between the *tart au citron* (topped with a meringue toupee) and the multi-layered *millefeuille*. In the end, I bought them both. Later, when I sat on a bench in Jardin du Luxembourg, I realized I had made the right choice.

A sliver of sunshine landed on me as I sat in the park, warming my cheeks. A few children were sailing toy sailboats in the fountain. A few men had hung their jackets on the racks (provided by the park) and had begun a game of *boules* nearby. I opened my notebook and scrounged around my bag for a pen.

Dear Áine,

I do a lot of walking in Paris. And on these walks, I come across plenty of statues. It's as though the city is standing guard, looking out pensively at something important in the distance. Some of these statues are heroic generals, revolutionaries, or kings on horses. Others are serene like the collection of queens and duchesses at Jardin du Luxembourg. Anne Marie Louise d'Orléans, Duchess of Montpensier, was one of the greatest heiresses in history. She was a defiant young lady, refusing a string of proposals from European ruling families and wanting only to marry for love. When she was refused, she opted out of the scene and died unmarried and childless. Many admire her for her strength, but I like her because she is situated under a shady tree and looks out to a grand fountain where children sail toy boats.

We spend a lot of time together, the duchess and I. She scored an excellent spot in the park—a nice trifecta of shade, people-watching, and silence. The fountain drowns out the sounds of nearby traffic, pierced only with the occasional police siren, which I don't mind because it reminds me of Jason Bourne movies. James Bond movies too.

The duchess doesn't do as much exploring as I do around Paris, preferring to stay put as statues are wont to do. By the time I reach her, my dogs are barking, and I pull up a chair to rest my feet.

We all must find places to explore in this world, but also places to rest. Paris is good about this. It's easy to walk for hours. Once you've lost your way or your spunk, you'll likely find a bench to sit and take a breather.

The guy sitting near to me is reading Le Monde, *the big French newspaper. There is a couple nearby reading a map. And dogs. A healthy population of prancing pups. There aren't as many poodles as I thought there would be, which suits me just fine. Pugs are the dog du jour these days. Their snorting makes me crack a smile every time. Not the duchess though. She's as serious as always, keeping guard over Paris, and perhaps me too, as I write this letter to you.*

À bientôt!
Janice

As I rose from my chair near the duchess, I noticed some meringue clinging to the inside of the dessert box. I scooped it up with my finger and popped it in my mouth. I realized I hadn't done this since I was a kid. In California, I didn't eat dessert, or even bread. Carbs were the devil in Los Angeles. Meals were vegetable-based and came in cardboard boxes from Whole Foods. I didn't cook; I assembled. If I was eating with someone, I assembled the boxed food on our plates. If I was alone, I skipped the plate. But here in Paris, the salad bars and bread ban—like the vegan thing—had been forgotten.

After my dessert in the park, I meandered back down rue Mouffetard. Before I turned right down my street, I slowed my gait near the butcher, who was stirring the potatoes that were roasting and collecting the drippings from the rotisserie of chickens above.

"*Bonjour, monsieur.*" I smiled. I added *monsieur* to my *repertoire.*

"*Bonjour, mademoiselle.*" He smiled.

I skipped to the door of my building. Is there anything more glorious than new crushes on boys? I opened the door with a code, walked into the foyer, and groped along the wall for the light switch. The foyer was lined with mailboxes, but of course there was no mail for me.

That was all done now.

11

Try Something New

There are times when I try the patience of my older sister. Three weeks into my time in Paris, there was a discernible undertone of exasperation in Julie's voice. I had been giving her daily updates from Paris about this butcher I'd been eyeing. I told her he looked like Daniel Craig. I told her we stared at each other.

"But you haven't told me if you have *talked* to him?"

Silence.

"You know how to speak French, Janice. You know grade-four French." Sheepishly, I admit that I took many, many classes all the way through high school. I even took night classes when I moved to California because I thought it was cool to take night classes at THE *Beverly Hills 90210* high school. And yet, the fear of speaking French to another person who speaks French had rendered me mute in Paris.

"Lesson one in grade-four French," my sister began. "*Bonjour. Je m'appelle Janice. Comment t'appelles-tu?*" Hello, my name is Janice. What is your name?

"Sounds simple enough."

"That's how you start speaking French." Exasperation spitting through the phone. "You. Start. Speaking. French." My sister has always had a flair for common sense, which is probably why I generally do what she says.

One day a few years ago, I was visiting her in Canada. My niece came home one day after school and complained that she felt bossed around on the playground. Julie said, "Next time, you tell those kids that they are not the boss of you. Mommy is the boss of you." My niece looked at me for further validation. I nodded. "Your mommy has been the boss of me my whole life. I don't mind. She's good at it."

So the next morning, I did as I was told and walked up to the butcher.

"*Bonjour, monsieur,*" I said.

"*Bonjour, mademoiselle,*" he replied.

"*Je m'appelle Janice. Comment t'appelles-tu?*"

"*Je m'appelle Christophe.*" And he pointed at my necklace, which had hanging from it my Saint Christopher's medal.

"*Tu parles anglais?*" I asked. Do you speak English?

"*Non.*"

Merde.

"*Ça va?*" How are you?

"*Ça va.*" I'm fine.

As I turned to leave, he touched my arm. I looked up at him.

"*Demain?*" he asked. Tomorrow?

"*Demain.*" I smiled.

Each day thereafter, I would walk up to him and say something in French that I had pieced together and rehearsed with help from Google Translate. I would see him in the morning and practice my future tense. "Today *I am going* to Musée Carnavalet. After, *I am going* to walk around Saint-Germain-des-Prés." He would nod, smile, and tell me to have a nice day. At the end of a day filled with crêpes, photo-taking, and navigation, I would walk up to him and practice my *passé composé*. "Today *I went* to Musée Carnavalet. After, *I walked* around Saint-Germain-des-Prés." And each day, he would nod and say, "*À demain?*" See you tomorrow? And I would say, "*À demain.*" See you tomorrow.

Then I'd walk home, stroking my Saint Christopher's medal, and watch the video I took of the butcher with my phone one morning from the café like I was a crazy stalker lady.

He probably went home thinking I was slow. Cute, but slow.

During my fourth week in Paris, I met up with my Uncle Brad and Aunt Mary. They were in town for a week to celebrate her retirement. When I was twelve years old, I took the train into Toronto with my sister to visit our uncle and aunt. It was our first trip away from our home in Clear Creek, Ontario, a small village on the edge of Lake Erie. He walked us around the city with a map and taught us how to navigate our way. "Always remember your compass directions," he said. "Internalize them. Know where the water is in reference to where you are going. That way, you'll be able to find your way back. You'll feel the freedom of exploring without fearing being lost." He pointed at the map. "You'll get lost, but you'll have confidence that you can get back on track again." This lesson came in handy in Paris as the three of us repeatedly got lost, but being lost in Paris was a joy. That's how we found an old instrument repair shop run by a man with a handlebar moustache, the bookbinding studio that dealt in restoration of old texts, and a candy shop where we found the most heavenly candies of unusual flavor combinations. None of these places were on the well-beaten path.

On one of our final mornings together, we headed toward Sainte-Chapelle, the glass cathedral that was the private cathedral of King Louis IX of France (the one who became a saint later). As we sat under the rainbow rays pouring through the stained glass, Uncle Brad told me about his Baptist upbringing and how he never felt any connection to God in church, but when he saw art, he felt something. "Art is a spiritual practice," he reflected. "If it weren't for art, I'd have given up on God a long time ago. This cathedral though"—he looked up at the walls of stained glass—"is very convincing."

We left the cathedral and walked through the Jardin des

Tuileries to the Musée de l'Orangerie to see Monet's *Nymphéas* (Water Lilies), which he painted in his garden in Giverny. This isn't one painting. It is a collection of murals lining large empty oval rooms. Talking in this room was discouraged, and I understood why the moment I arrived. The air was thick with calm and peace. It was as if we left our words in the coat check. I sat next to my Aunt Mary. She leaned over and whispered, "Feel it?" I nodded. It was the moment I began to fall in love with silence.

After the museum, we strolled over to the Jardin des Tuileries for a picnic. With the warm April sun on us, we unraveled the contents of our bags and grabbed four of the hundreds of olive green chairs strewn about: three for sitting and one to use as the table. We made sandwiches of various charcuterie meats and cheeses. I peeled the top slice of salami from the stack. My aunt said, "I thought you were vegetarian."

"Worse," I replied. "Vegan."

"With the cheese they have around here?" She cut off a small triangle of creamy chèvre and popped it in her mouth. "That's sacrilege."

I told my aunt and uncle about the butcher and how I felt like I was talking to him like a three-year-old, that speaking French was too hard, that he was too hard to get to know.

"Act like a fool, sound terrible, and make laughable grammatical errors," said my uncle. He was a primary school teacher in Toronto. He taught English to many immigrant children. "Act like a child."

So on the days that followed, I continued talking to my butcher friend, making grammatical errors and sounding foolish along the way. He replied in slow French, smiling and likely holding back laughter, but he was still a stranger, which made acting like a fool feel somewhat okay.

One evening, I was heading to an English-speaking Meetup group for expats. There are hundreds of these specialized groups all over Paris. A friend once said, "If you're an expat lesbian tightrope walker in Paris, there is a Meetup group for you."

Now I'm not one to go out on a limb and meet people. I'm introverted, and crowds exhaust me. But sometimes you have to be the grown-up of your life and tell your inner child, who is kicking and screaming, "Get your shoes on. This is not optional. We have a play date."

So that's what I did. I put on my shoes and started walking up the street to the Meetup group. Insolent and begrudging.

But who should be sitting in a bar up the street? Why, it was Christophe, wasn't it? And didn't he see me just as I was walking by? Why yes, he did. And didn't he jump up from his bar stool and rush outside to ask me if I would be interested in having a drink? Why yes, he did.

But he did it in very few words. He pointed at the bar and said, "*Bière?*" Lucky for him, I'm Canadian and know the French word for beer. And lucky for me, when I saddled up to the bar with Christophe, all the bartenders were Canadian and bilingual. Oh God in Heaven, thank you for this moment.

Teaming up with the bartenders, we managed to piece together a Franglish conversation of sorts. They were determined to help their friend pick up this Canadian girl. And when no one was looking, I asked Christophe if I could take a photo of him and me. You know, the kind where you are cheek to cheek and one of you has your arms outstretched with the camera to get the photo. And that's when he turned and kissed me!

Cue sexy smooching scene. On film even!

He immediately pulled back and apologized. "*Désolé, désolé, désolé.*" Sorry, sorry, sorry.

I immediately leaned in and said, "*Non désolé, non désolé, non désolé.*" No sorry, no sorry, no sorry. It wasn't my most elegant speech, but he understood.

I never did make it to the Meetup group.

Instead I walked around Paris with Christophe for half the

night, with stops here and there for late-night coffees and smooches. The cafés were crowded. The streets pulsed with the heat of spring sunlight earlier that day. When he dropped me off at my building, I pointed up to show him the windows of the apartment where I was staying. He kissed me good-bye and said something to me in French. I'm not sure what it was, but I hoped it was something nice. It certainly seemed like something nice by the way he said it.

The next day, I walked by the butcher shop, and he said something in French that I didn't understand, but it had an inflection at the end of the sentence that led me to believe he asked me a question. Hoping he had just asked me out, I responded in French with my rehearsed, "My window tonight at 8:30?" He nodded. That night when I looked out my window at 8:30, he was standing there ready for our date. And he was standing there every night at 8:30 for the next two weeks, which were also what I thought would be the last two weeks of my time in the city.

Cue sexy love affair in Paris.

How long does one wait to have sex with a cute butcher in Paris? In my old life, I would have held out as per the rules in ladies magazines, and honestly, most of the men gave up right around the time I was buying undies for the big event. But the code of conduct is different for a traveler. Travelers live by this rule: collect as many experiences as you can without getting yourself killed *or worse*.

So how long does a traveler wait? Evidently not long. This was new for me. I used to watch *Sex and the City* and wonder if every girl was getting it on all time, because I wasn't and neither were my friends. We weren't nuns, for heaven's sake, but we weren't so…slutty either. And most of us were mystified by the amount of sex Carrie and her gaggle of girlfriends had with the boys of New York. But with Christophe, I must admit I deliberately didn't wait, simply because I was running out of time. Would it end in heartbreak? Likely. Would I look back on it fondly? Definitely.

All the aches and pains in my calloused heart had been replaced by soft touches and smooches here and there. And *there*. And a few nights after our first date in the bar, he reached a part of me inside that had been silent too long. In ecstasy, she screamed out for more.

12

Mona Lisa Smile

I spent my final weeks in Paris with Christophe. Before I came strolling down the rue, he had booked a vacation to Poland. I learned that my French butcher boyfriend wasn't French at all. He was from a small city in Poland. He called the airline and his brother a few days before his flight and said he wouldn't be going. He had to see about a girl.

The lease on my dank flat was up, and I moved into a hotel for the final three days. Christophe moved in with me, and we spent most of our time honeymooning in our robes, interrupted by occasional walks along the Seine and meals at bistros. Because we couldn't speak the same language, we walked in silence much of the time. In the silence, holding hands or with his strong arm around my shoulder, we became part of the city, feeling it in the moment: watching boats slowly coast beneath the bridges, standing beneath trees that were now raining down blossoms in the breeze, sitting at cafés and watching the world stroll by.

Who was this guy? What was his story? I didn't know and didn't have the language skills to find out. I had to rely on other clues to discover more about Christophe. He was always on time, he always opened the door for me, and he was tender, strong, and considerate. He showered me with kisses and hugs, and he constantly asked if I needed anything. I could usually only respond with simple *Oui* or *Non*, which seemed to be enough for him. We had our own versions of charades and Pictionary to communicate. We'd point and nod. Sublanguages ruled.

Turns out guys love when chicks don't talk their ears off. Had I played the W.A.I.T. game (Why Am I Talking) like this back in Los Angeles, would I have found love? My friend Áine always finds love in foreign lands. There seems to be an energy shift that opens her up to love. Was it just because she couldn't speak the language as well as a native speaker who could rattle on? Was this what was happening to me?

Christophe and I lived in the present, which is the only tense in French I could muddle through with a modicum of success. As we walked, I would look for scenes to photograph. He would look at me. During this time, I felt freer than ever before. Without the ability to tell him my backstory, I was just Janice In Paris. No one else. I was not a tired corporate drone. I was not a direct marketing professional. I was not the story of who I was the year before, secretly plotting my escape from corporate life. As for his backstory, as I ran my fingers up and down his chest and legs, I felt a scar here and there. I'd ask him what it was. "Accident," he'd reply. "Fall. Bad." I would nod, knowing all I needed to know for now.

I couldn't project any pressure onto him about the future, not only because I didn't have the language skills to hint, but also because we both knew the score. I was traveling through town. For all I knew, he could have been like the many men in France who are very happy to accommodate women who are, for the first time, discovering the traveler's code of conduct. A drink here, help with a map in broken English, a grateful woman who loves the sound of an accent. After one or two hot, unforgettable nights, she can skip off into the sunset, back to her regularly scheduled life, and stalk him on Facebook with her reliable speedy Internet service back home.

In the mornings, I would plan the itinerary, pulling out my maps and notes. I would point. *I've got to see this and that and this and that.* Busy, busy, busy, always running. Christophe would nod at my plan. "You want?" he would say. I would nod. "Maybe one." And then I'd pick a place on my list and we'd go. Before Christophe came along, I was a workaholic tourist. Fast. Go. Get there. See it all. Take loads of photos *just in case.* Go, go, go. But Christophe, he had more of a saunter. And with him always holding my hand and never letting go, I could either drag him along or let him set the pace. There were times when I had been fighting my way through a pack of tourists at Notre Dame and I forgot to look at the cathedral altogether, but with him setting the pace, I could see layers of the city I missed before when I was running to catch the green lights. I thought I knew Paris fairly well by now, but with Christophe leading the way, I was led to small interesting pockets. I soon realized that Paris isn't just a big city; it's a series of small communities as well.

A few months before, just after I bought my plane ticket to Paris, I fantasized about speaking French and buying a baguette on the walk home. I dreamed of sitting in cafés like they do in postcards. Now here I was, doing all this hand-in-hand with the lovely Christophe. I could hardly believe what was happening to me.

On a cold, gray day in April, we opted to visit the Louvre. I had been there three weeks prior to see the *pièce de résistance,* the *Mona Lisa,* and quite honestly, I didn't get what all the fuss was about. On my first viewing of the world's most recognized painting, I was slightly disappointed. It was smaller than I imagined, a mere 30 x 21 inches. It was dark and drab and not nearly as jaw-dropping as many of the other masterpieces surrounding it. I needed another look, and Christophe was game. Immediately after buying our tickets from a vending machine beneath I. M. Pei's pyramid, I grabbed his hand and tried to fight the crowds who were also heading toward the painting that made Dan Brown famous. He kept pulling me back to look at the art *en route*. I started feeling panicked that I would run out of museum-going mojo by the time we arrived at the painting, but he had no such thoughts. He wanted to stroll and pause, stroll and pause. I breathed deep and checked in with myself before addressing his snail's pace.

She's not going anywhere.

Mr. Miyagi, in his infinite wisdom, was right once again. Mona Lisa wasn't leaving the building. She wasn't touring the earth. She was staying put. I could take my time. And when I took a deep breath, stopped trying to drag Christophe through the crowd, I understood what made this museum special. I saw the sculptures, pillaged by centuries of kings, exquisite paintings traded and bought, stolen and found from around the world, and I saw the intricate décor along the grand walls of the palace itself. A fine place for royalty and emperors to call home. The art *before* arriving at the *Mona Lisa* was quite lovely. Who knew? I didn't even see it the first time.

Before long, I was back at the *Mona Lisa* for another look at her enigmatic smile. I had done some research and knew that the way she was painted became the standard for how portraits would be painted and photos (once photography was invented) would be taken henceforth. Before the *Mona Lisa*, paintings were full-length profiles looking in the distance with the background being as clear as the foreground. She had a three-quarter-length pose, looked directly at the painter, and is in front of a background that faded in the distance. She also had no outlines around her eyes and mouth, which made her even more realistic.

Oh, how far we've come. Now we can re-create the same look with a photo app on our phones!

With Christophe at my side, we stood before the lovely Lisa del Giocondo to see what all the fuss was about. I stared and stared. What was it with this lady? I kept looking at this mysterious smile. I kept forgetting that this was a painting. The lines blended so well that I couldn't see paint strokes, which was a new technique at the time. What was she trying to convey? What was he, Leonardo da Vinci, trying to convey. She. He. She. He.

Then it hit me.

This smile is the smile of someone who was treated well by others...but more importantly, by herself. She was pleased with her life and it showed, or glowed, to be more precise. She radiated serenity. The same glow I've seen on old ladies watching over grandchildren in the park. The glow of yogis after a meditation. The glow I've seen on myself in the mirror the mornings after nights with Christophe.

I could have been projecting all this onto the lovely lady who sat composed in her kind silence in front of me. The first time I saw her, I didn't see any of this. I saw the crowds gathered that I had to fight through as if I were in a car on the freeway back in Los Angeles. Fighting traffic on-road and off. But now that I had experienced more than a week of vacation, a juicy love affair, and eaten the most luscious food of my life, I was developing my own Mona Lisa smile.

And da Vinci saw this and painted it! Amazing.

I nodded to Christophe. He nodded back and pointed at the Egyptian collection on the map. I nodded, and we sauntered slowly toward the mummies. Later at the gift shop, I bought a print of my new friend Mona and tucked her in my journal like some people tuck cards of saints or gurus in their wallets. A reminder to aim for that feeling on my journey.

When we had seen enough, we sauntered back to the hotel to make soup and love. "You want?" he said and eyed the bed. I want. And we made love very slowly. As he held me, he told me that with everyone he was closed but with me he was open.

Well, that was something. Without my ability to tell the stories of my past, I felt more closed than ever. But maybe that was a good thing. Maybe we weren't our stories. Those could be events, memories, and lessons, but not necessarily definitions of self.

We stayed up most of my last three nights in Paris. Talking slowly, kissing slowly, touching, and caressing. There was nowhere else to be, nothing more to do, no more tourist attractions to add to my list. There was no list. There was no email to check, no one that required anything from me other than a Mona Lisa smile. Up until that point, those were the sexiest nights of my life.

On our final day, we boarded the train that would take me to the airport and away from my French-speaking Polish lover. At the airport, as we waited for my check-in line to open, he fetched coffees while I stood with the luggage. In the two minutes alone, I cried and couldn't quite compose myself by the time he returned. Would I ever come back? I had told him I had a return ticket from Paris to Canada for a few months later and I would call. He smiled, wiped my tears away, and said he would call every day. I pushed the torrent down. Wait until the plane. The hotel. Just wait. He said he loved me. I said I loved him. Whether or not it was true wasn't important. What was important was that we knew how to say it in French and English. During the two weeks together, we filled a lot of space with *je t'aimes*, and I wondered in the silence of my own mind whether it was true or not. But for now, for these two weeks, I could say it and let it be the intense love affair that it was.

As we stood near the security line, he asked me to promise him something. I had no idea what he had asked. "*Oui, je promise, je promise, je promise.*" Then I paused and asked him what I was promising. We laughed, both of us knowing that time and plane tickets can void any promises to ride off into the sunset together.

It was time. He kissed and hugged me in a way that made me forget the concepts of time, space, and circumstance. In his arms, I was in an eternal space where I craved to be forever. A man's love. I got it. I really got it. For two weeks, I really got what I hadn't been getting until this beautiful creature showed me. He never, ever kept me guessing. He never, ever kept me waiting. He always showed up.

He kissed me on the forehead and said, "Go." I nodded, turned, and slowly walked toward the security line, knowing he was watching me. I turned even though they all say you shouldn't. I was right. He was standing there looking at me with the same curious glance he'd had all those mornings when I sat at the café and he stood at the butcher shop. I blew him a kiss. He smiled, caught it with his hand, and held it to his heart. I walked through Security and looked for signs to my gate.

In my old life, I would have spent a week sniffling on the couch over my lost love. But in my traveler's life, I had to compartmentalize feelings. When I was on the move, there was little room for emotional breakdowns. There were too many signs to read, too many physical needs to meet—finding shelter, food, hotels, and gates. So with the exception of that two-minute burst of tears before getting on the plane, I was calm and cool. Once seated, I waited for whatever I had choked down to come up.

But nothing came. Instead, as the plane took off, I looked through the window at the fields below and thought back to my time with Christophe—his hands, his lips, his eyes. I caught my reflection in the glass and saw that I was smiling. I recognized the look.

13

Declare Nothing but Your Genius

The Customs line at the airport in Edinburgh read, "Nothing to declare."

I was so very happy to be in a Customs line with an English-speaking Customs agent that when he asked me if I had anything to declare, I wanted to sing out a quote from Oscar Wilde, "I have nothing to declare but my genius." But I didn't. You don't joke with the Customs guy, for fear of saying something irreversible. (I have always felt mildly guilty at Customs. I have to keep telling myself that I did nothing wrong. I was innocent. I didn't even buy Duty Free). The Customs agent looked at my passport. "MacLeod of the Clan MacLeod." Has every man in the world watched *The Highlander*? Is there some kind of specialized training for men? Because every man I met along the way referred to me as "MacLeod of the Clan MacLeod."

"Yes," I replied, probably a little too seriously.

"Does this mean you're immortal too?" he questioned.

Was he serious? "I believe so," I replied. "Only time will tell."

He laughed and asked me if I was in the country on business.

I laughed back, thinking the ice was broken. "No, I am not here on business. I am delighted to report that I have no business being here at all." I should have stopped there. "I'm floating through Europe, twirling and whirling and seeing and doing and definitely not working."

He stopped laughing. He probably thought I was slow. Cute, but slow.

I dropped off my suitcase at the hotel and peeled off to find a traditional Scottish breakfast. I found a pub whose menu read: "A classic Scottish breakfast with sausage, smoked back bacon, fried egg, potato scone, and slices of black pudding and haggis served with button mushrooms, whole oven-baked tomato, and baked beans."

I'll have one, please. Add a giant mug of coffee. It was nice to move on from the thimble-size espresso of Paris. When the heaping platter arrived, I laughed, seeing just how far I'd gone from veganism. I picked up my fork and began chipping away at the feast.

With breakfast sloshing in my belly, I wobbled up a street pockmarked with tourist shops leading to the castle. Edinburgh is a beautiful Scottish city, and it's even more beautiful in spring. I couldn't believe my timing. Just as the last of the blossoms had tumbled down from the trees in Paris, I arrived in Edinburgh to relive them all.

I immediately fell back into my overachieving, fast-paced tourist ways. I toured the kilt factory. Check! (I'm sorry to say that my MacLeod tartan is a very loud bumblebee yellow. I settled on the "Thistle" pattern, a gray-and-black little number with pink stripes that went well with the rest of my wardrobe, which is Catholic schoolgirl in nature. Not really. But now, all I needed was a Ramones T-shirt and I would look like all the teens around here. What is with Ramones T-shirts?)

I researched my ancestors. Check! I stormed the castle. Ready, set, charge! I rented the audio tour and began climbing up the hill to find out more about this castle. Halfway up, listening to facts ramble in my ear, I was hit with Fact Fatigue. After listening to and reading facts about Paris for six weeks, I'd reached my limit just about the time I got to the castle. I did my best to be interested in the big showcase story of the castle: the crown jewels and how they got there. Basically, like every other set of crown jewels gets anywhere. Smuggling, stealing, presenting, and repeating until someone installs a security system, and even then it's all a crapshoot.

Speaking of...

ATTN: Asshole Hotel in Edinburgh

To whom it may concern:

When I was looking for a hotel in your fair city of Edinburgh, I had certain requirements. I was looking for something centrally located. Your hotel is certainly in the city center. I was looking for Internet access, which you provide at a pirate's rate of $20 per day. And I was looking for clean lodgings. I admit, though the place is somewhat run-down and in need of a facelift, it's clean.

I didn't think that toilets that work should have been added to the list of amenities I was looking for in a hotel. The first room I had was equipped with a faulty toilet. Fine. These things happen. How would you know it was broken if a guest didn't report it? And you were kind to give me another room.

But when I flushed in my new room, it didn't work either. I mean, c'mon.

I'd flush and get a trickle for my efforts. I'd flush again. Trickle again. Then I became like a Pavlovian dog, flushing the toilet again and again, hoping the incessant pushing of the handle would culminate in one successful flush.

At one point, I shut the lid, sat down, opened a magazine, and read two full articles while I flushed repeatedly with the other hand. Eventually, and this is probably on flush thirty, I had success.

Thirty flushes doth not a working toilet make.

And just so you know, I'm talking about "Number 1" here. When faced with a defective toilet? Forget the other option. Scared like a turtle.

AND I HAD THE TRADITIONAL SCOTTISH BREAKFAST.

The clincher came when I checked out of this hotel and mentioned the toilet issue yet again to the receptionist. "Yes," she said. "We have many complaints about the toilets." Then. Do. Something. About. It.

"Yes, yes. Sometimes we have to send a porter up to help people with the toilets." I can just imagine that scene.

No, no. No. Your hotel sucks. Obviously.

Seriously,

Janice MacLeod (of the clan MacLeod)

After two days in Edinburgh, I hopped a train to Glasgow. I was relieved when I arrived at my beautiful hotel. I soon realized that there wasn't much in the way of touristy things to do in Glasgow. I'm not knocking the city by saying this. I was actually delighted to be let off the hook and not feel required to do a lot of site-seeing. Or is it sight-seeing? Either way, I didn't do any of it.

Instead, I took time out of my busy tourist schedule to chill and ponder what exactly happened in Paris with Christophe. He'd emailed and Skyped daily since I left. He called and sent texts. Without hand signals and facial clues, it was even more challenging to talk. And I couldn't always hear him on Skype. I would just talk into cyberspace, not knowing if he could hear me. Some of these calls would end with a crackly *je t'aime* or the line would go dead mid-sentence and the connection wouldn't come back.

I sent him many photos of my swanky citizenM hotel room in Glasgow. This was a discount hotel but was so smartly designed that I would choose a room here before many other luxury hotels. citizenM was like The W hotel for people on a budget. The room was clean. The bed was big, and beside it was a port for your phone so you could listen to your own music while charging up. There were no dressers because they know people only stay for a night or two and rarely unpack their suitcase. And I am happy to report that the toilets worked just fine.

I think I watched ten episodes of *Friends* in *English* in my hotel room. They LOVE *Friends* here, and I say do as the locals do. I also went to the drug store (how I love Boots), took care of my postal needs at the post office, and bought new running shoes, as I had worn mine out traipsing around Paris.

As I drifted to sleep in between episodes of *Friends*, I thought back to Christophe. I was surprised to find that my memories of our time together in Paris didn't fade. On the contrary, they became more vivid. All the details floated through my head. His lips on my neck, his arm around my waist, the smell of his skin—they were part of my body now. Only geography separated us.

After two days of acting like a local by running errands, I took another swipe at my suitcase before I boarded my next train. My winter clothes had to go. I was heading south from here, and spring was turning into summer. Then came the Corporate Barbie pants. I am sorry to report that they came along with me to Paris and Scotland. What was I thinking? There is more to life than slimming black slacks. I tossed them in the trash bin. I exhaled and smiled. I was sloughing off my old life with every day I was in my new life.

My cousin fetched me on the train platform in Yorkshire Dales. We drove along winding roads through the hilly countryside speckled with grazing sheep. We arrived at her cottage in Kirkby Lonsdale. The cottage was crammed with teacups and books, and the walls were lined with artwork. This artwork caught my eye. They were actually letters with paintings on them. Or paintings with writing on them. They were addressed to Joan, the owner of the house, and were created by the English artist Percy Kelly.

Joan and Percy Kelly were pen pals during the 1980s. She discovered his watercolor paintings in a gallery and sent him a letter, asking if he would show her more of his works. He responded with a painted letter. Joan, delighted by the stunning letter, wrote him back immediately. And he wrote back with another equally beautiful painted letter. So she wrote back and he wrote back. A deep friendship commenced, and ten years of letters from Percy Kelly arrived in her mailbox.

For much of that time, they wrote two or three letters a week, most of which depicted scenes from his memories of living in Cumbria and Pembrokeshire, plus scenes from where he lived in Norfolk. (Incidentally, the county where I am from in Canada is also called Norfolk.) He died penniless, largely because he couldn't bear to sell most of his paintings. He only held five art shows in his life and not-for-sale works dominated them. He claimed the art was too important to him. The love ran too deep.

As I read the letters, I understood what he meant by love. I started falling in love with the letters too. I felt like I was snooping through someone else's mail. His paintings were brilliant, but his writing was humdrum.

After his death, Joan compiled and displayed his letters in galleries. Whenever they weren't on public display, they decorated the walls of her house. I also found anthologies of his work in the bookshelves. Since the collection of letters was so vast (about 1,600), I was able to study how Percy created these pieces. I even felt like Percy was showing me how.

I hadn't done any painting while I had been on the road. Now, I was in England and yearning to paint again. Along came Percy Kelly to show me how I could do it on my nomadic journey. I didn't have room in my luggage for canvases, but he showed me a medium that makes sense for a traveler (letters), and in his letters, he described what he used: a small basic watercolor kit and whatever paper he found. Simple. Beautiful. Doable.

Many days during my week in the English countryside, I sat in a chair with Percy's book. At moments, I felt Percy whispering to me from the pages.

This is how I started this painting, right here at this line. See how it's the strongest. This was the second line I drew, and the third. Then I fleshed it out from there. Notice how I simplified and faded the drawing here so I could add text. And look at where I let the pen ink mix with the paint here to capture the mood of the scene.

Little whispers from beyond to show me the way.

In an old stone store around the corner from the cottage, I found a small set of watercolors. I packed it in my suitcase, hugged my cousin good-bye, and headed to London. From the train platform, I called Grant, with whom I was staying, to let him know I was on my way.

"I'll be here," he said. "Ben will be here too. How amazing is that? All the way from Los Angeles." Ben. Oh my stars.

Soon after, Ben had sent me a message. We had arranged to meet at Kensal Green platform and walk to Grant's house together. I had arrived a few minutes before him. He stepped off the platform. We hugged, did a happy dance, and walked slowly to the house. We talked about our time together in Los Angeles and how we championed each other during our escape plans. He was in London to finesse the details about becoming the opening act for a few big tours around Europe. I had left my job and made it to Europe. Life was happening.

Once Grant went to bed and I was alone again with Ben, I asked him what to do about Christophe. He looked at me like I was insane. "Go to him! See where it leads. This is why you did this. You may not have realized it at the time. You thought you were just looking to quit your job, but really, you were looking for happiness. You could find it with Christophe. What could happen? Happiness? Great. Ruin? You can handle that. Do you think you'll lose everything and become homeless? You already got rid of everything. You're already homeless."

I exhaled and sang a few lines from "Me and Bobby McGee": "Freedom's just another word for nothing left to lose."

He continued. "And nothin' ain't worth nothin' but it's

free." He looked me. "You think we'll ever sing up every song we ever knew?"

"With them windshield wipers slappin' time?" I sang. "It's possible."

He sighed heavily, looked up, and sang: "Somewhere near Salinas, Lord, I let her slip away."

We were silent, allowing this reality to sink in.

He said, "You think it was a past life thing?"

"Who knows? Maybe all our coffee shop visits happened just so we could have this moment right here and now so you could tell me what to do."

"Nothing more?" he asked.

"*Early Show.*"

He nodded. "*Late Night.* Maybe you and I were never meant to fully run our course. Never meant to falter or fade." He paused. "Or feel like it's too late."

"It's late. I'm going to bed."

He sang Aerosmith: "I don't want to close my eyes. I don't want to fall asleep, I'd still miss you, baby, and I don't want to miss a thing." He stopped singing. "Maybe all the girls in my life end up as sad love songs."

We sat with this thought for a minute. He turned to me, held my hand, and said, "You broke my heart when you left California."

"Ben."

"No, no. No. You don't have to explain." He shrugged. "*C'est la vie.*"

Ben's arrival turned out to be more than just good timing. I had questions that only a friend who knows the long version of my life's story could answer. I also needed to know where to go in Italy. He was a seasoned traveler and great with advice. He was clear and spoke like a loving, bossy, older brother. I got out my map.

He pointed here and there. "This is what you're going to do and this is what you're not going to do." He laid out the next leg of my travel plan for me: Rome, Florence, Venice, and if I knew what was good for me, Paris.

Dear Áine,

The royal wedding made every girl feel like a princess. The street vendors made sure of that by selling thousands of tiaras to the throngs that arrived in London for the big day. There is nothing like seeing a grandma and a little girl both wear tiaras together, walking down the Mall, hoping to catch a glimpse of the carriage with the new royal couple. The parks were outfitted with massive screens so we could all watch the ceremony along with those watching in living rooms around the world. Sitting there waving Union Jacks as the wedding was about to begin, people started shushing really loudly. A mild murmur ensued. But in that moment when William and Harry stepped out of the car, the crowd erupted in cheers. Followed soon after by more shushing, followed again by loud cheers when Kate stepped out of her car.

The ceremony was, of course, glorious, romantic, and proper, from what I could tell from a crowd one hundred people deep. Once they were officially hitched, in the carriage heading back to Buckingham, the crowds shuffled in that direction too, to catch the kiss.

The real fun came afterward. Pubs were decked out with flags and streamers. Some even served wedding cake. And by the end of the night, even the guys were wearing tiaras.

Ah, the romance of it all.

Next stop, Rome. Oh my dear, how will I manage Rome without you?

Janice

14

There Is No Place Like Rome

As I waited for my baggage at Fiumicino Airport in Rome, the lovely Christophe emailed me a cryptic Google Translated message, introducing the idea of coming back to Paris to stay with him for the summer "to see." Though this was appealing, it would be the first time I'd lived with a boy. And call me old-fashioned, but I was sort of saving myself for someone, in that way. I figured I should save *something*. I chewed on this thought for a long time as I stood by the carousel. I stood too long, in fact. Where the hell was my bag?

There is always that moment. You're at baggage claim waiting for your luggage. And waiting. And waiting. Everyone else has left with their bags. You seethe with jealousy and worry. Then the conveyor belt stops. No bag for you.

When you only have one suitcase and that suitcase is gone, you don't even freak out and blame the airline. You immediately point a finger to the heavens, curse God, and storm off to the baggage claim desk. Once I managed to successfully convey the color and size of my suitcase to the claims agent, I grabbed a cab to the Pantheon.

Italians are crazy drivers. My driver whipped us around ruins and scooters and little old ladies carrying sacks of tomatoes. He swung around the Pantheon and screeched to a halt at the address where I would be staying for the next few weeks. The rental agent was leaning on the wall next to the door, helmet in one hand, keys in the other. He was wearing designer jeans, a leather jacket, and had one curl falling down the front of his forehead. He could have been in *Grease*. He almost looked like he was *posing*. We shook hands as is my custom, and he kissed me on both cheeks as is his custom. We walked up the six flights to my apartment. When I saw that it was bright, clean, and similar to the photos I'd seen online, I handed over the other half of the deposit and bid him a cheery *ciao*. I sat on the edge of the bed and looked around. This would have been the moment I unpacked. But without a suitcase... I grinned and grabbed my purse. I bounded back down those six flights of stairs and hit the street in search of clothes.

Oh, the joy of *having* to buy clothes again. I had no choice. I only had what was on my back. For over a year, I had turned a blind eye to fashion, not wanting to be tempted to buy more than I could carry. But on my first day in Rome, I meandered down ivy-lined alleyways to small boutiques filled with pretty summer dresses and shiny shoes. I found the perfect pink wrap-around dress and ballet flats. My first new outfit in Europe. Actually, my first new outfit in ages. I was in love. Good thing, too, because I had to live in it for the next few days. I surprised myself by being okay with this fact. When my luggage finally arrived three days later, I realized that I didn't need to lug around nearly as much, so I got busy decluttering once again. More of my clothes went into the trash. I was left with only the few clothes I absolutely loved. The others? I never chose them anyway, yet I insisted on lugging them around with me. With only the clothes I loved, I was set.

Nervously ironing out invisible wrinkles in my dress, I was standing behind the gate to the left of Saint Peter's Basilica, where I was to meet Marco. This time, we would be alone. What exactly had I promised him last May when he whispered

Promettimi che ritornerò? And what had I promised Christophe before I left Paris?

Behind the gate were Swiss Guards, and in front of the gate were throngs of people milling about for the beatification of Pope John Paul II, his first step toward sainthood. His body was moved from the crypt below to five-star permanent residency in the main hall of Saint Peter's Basilica. But good Catholic that I am, I hadn't come to see the Pope. I came to see Marco.

Marco worked at the Vatican. He was one of the bodyguards to the Pope. During the Pope's daily constitutional walk, Marco was there. When the Pope sat in the Sistine Chapel for his morning prayers, Marco was there. When a tourist would get a little too close for comfort, Marco was there. How did he get this job? Apparently, this kind, soft-spoken, beautiful Roman man had a handful of black belts and could knock your block off before you knew your block was knocked off.

Soon he waltzed through the line of Swiss guards and whispered in the ear of the man at the gate. He pointed to me, and the man opened the gate to usher me in. The onlookers stood agape with eyes and mouths wide open. *How did she get in? Who is she?*

You know that final scene in *An Officer and a Gentleman*? The one where Richard Gere walks into the factory in his uniform, scoops up Debra Winger, and carries her off to live happily ever after? That's how I felt when I saw Marco again.

Along with being handsome and sexy in his uniform, Marco was extremely kind. His heart was so big that I felt it radiating just by standing near him. I suppose that's what happens when you walk around the grounds with the Pope every morning while he does his rosary.

He gave me a big hug. "She returns to the scene of the crime."

"But we haven't done anything wrong yet."

He winks. "The day is young."

We picked up flirting right where we had left off last May

when I was in Rome with Áine. Looking back, it's tough to tell if he was flirting with me because he liked me or he was flirting with me because he was just so good at it. Why squelch a gift? My mind drifted to thoughts of Christophe, who didn't even know how flirty I could be because I couldn't flirt in French yet. But Marco spoke English.

I had had impure thoughts about Marco from the moment I met him. And yes, I returned to the scene anticipating a crime of sorts. Thinking of Marco gave me the strength in my final months of working in my advertising agency to listen to Italian language CDs and practice, practice, practice. I was hoping to return to Rome to find a manly man who could embrace me so that I felt both secure and adored. I had to win the affection of his mamma. I had to learn for which team to cheer. I had to practice my guitar so I could play love songs on Sunday afternoons for the family to win their affection—my humble apology for not being born Roman. I had to become the Canadian version of Penelope Cruz for these people. I had to make them love me.

So Marco was my first candidate, or at least he had been before Paris. My feelings were conflicted when I thought back to my blue-eyed butcher in Paris. We took the elevator to the roof of the basilica and walked toward the forbidden area lined with statues. A guard waved us through with a smile and a wink. Scores of people were milling about Saint Peter's Square. Looking down at them, I felt like royalty. I also felt like telling the crowds not to cry for me, Argentina. But no, no. No.

"Bella," Marco began as he put his arm around my shoulders. "I must tell you first that there is nothing more I want in this moment than to undo the tie on your beautiful pink dress. I might have even attempted it if this entire area was not being filmed on security cameras right now."

I felt excited yet uneasy about being monitored by people in a distant surveillance room who were likely wondering why Marco was up in the forbidden area with a girl.

Marco continued. "But you see, my dear, I have met some-one and have given her my heart. I have made a vow and," he waved his hand, "vows are not to be broken by men in my position." He looked down at the generous cleavage line on my dress. "But from this position, you are very difficult to resist."

At this point, I think I should have felt disappointment or sadness. My crush had found another girl. Instead, I felt relieved. I confessed. "I too have met someone in Paris," I said. "Now you and I know where we stand." And where we stood was right next to Michelangelo's statue of Jesus on the roof on Saint Peter's Basilica. "We will have to adore each other from afar and leave it at that."

"Perfect. Today, I will take you to the best *gelateria* in Rome, but you must promise to never tell anyone. I am accepting you as a Roman citizen, and we Romans don't share everything with the tourists."

I nodded. "Our secret."

"And if it pleases you, I will call Sandro and we will get paella for dinner tonight. You must meet his new girlfriend. She is just like Penelope Cruz."

Later, we nestled into a free corner on the stairs by Trevi Fountain and dug into our gelato. As I fell more deeply in love with every flavor, Marco explained how you could tell a lot about a person's love life by how they eat gelato.

He took a scoop of my lemon. "There are the Monday-Tuesday-Thursday-Wednesday types," he began. "These people eat gelato daily. They also like to make the love daily, or would if they could." He popped it in his mouth, closed his eyes, and sighed. When done, he took a scoop of his hazelnut and continued. "There are the Can't-Settle-Down types. These people taste a lot of flavors before settling on just one. Once they make a choice and walk away with their cone, they are still thinking of what other flavors are out there that they could experience." He continued. "I used to be like this, but I'm older and wiser now." He tried my pear. "That's good. The Shouldas are those who try a flavor but *shoulda* got the other one. These people live with regret. They probably regret most of their relationships."

"What if you have a favorite flavor?" I asked. "What's wrong with that? I cannot get enough of your hazelnut."

"These are the Monogamists. They found the one flavor that fills their heart with joy. They would eat this flavor every day if they could." He put his hand on my shoulder. "My dear, you didn't come to Rome to be a Monogamist, did you?"

I tried my strawberry. And his cherry. And his chocolate.

He smiled and continued. "Then there are the Observers. These are a rare but sad breed. They aren't eating, partaking, or even enjoying watching others partake in the gelato-eating orgy. I don't know how they live life, but they must be sad and lonely." We had finished our cups. Six flavors between the two of us. "And now, my dear. What does your gelato say about you?"

I pondered this for a minute and nodded. "I was a Monogamist on my first visit to Rome because I liked hazelnut so much, but now I'm clearly a Monday-Tuesday-Thursday-Wednesday type with Can't-Settle-Down tendencies. I'm not a Shouldas type, as everything I've tried has been fantastic, which is also true of my love life lately, come to think of it. And I know for sure that I can't be just an Observer."

He slapped my knee. "Good girl."

That night, we met up with Sandro at a restaurant on the edge of Piazza Navona. Over a steaming pan of paella, I told them my big news. That I had made a New Year's resolution last year to become an artist, but instead I quit my job and was now traveling indefinitely.

Sandro stared back in amazement. "*Non c'e terra che te regge.*" No soil can hold you.

Marco put down his fork. "To a Roman, you are both a hero and a fool."

"What do Romans dream about if not finding work that makes them happy?"

They howled with laughter at this. Sandro took my hand. "Janice, the only way to happiness is to find people with whom you can eat, drink, and laugh. That is all. That is everything." He added. "And a spoonful of Nutella each day makes life more beautiful. It's an antidepressant."

Sandro and Marco have had their jobs for years and plan on having them until they retire. Apparently, when someone gets a good job around here, they keep it as long as they can and they are grateful for it. For them, work is a way to afford life, but not a definition of who you are.

As a person who spent her career in advertising, the concept of keeping a job for life floors me. In advertising, we routinely move from agency to agency, city to city. If an agency loses an account, poof! You could be gone in as much time as it takes HR to do the paperwork. But after the initial awkward conversation with your boss and the strange feeling of a midday commute home, you bounce back relatively quickly. You send your resume to the ad agency that picked up the account your agency just lost, touting in the cover letter that you're best for the job and can help them ramp up, and boom, you're back in the game. Advertising people learn to roll with the punches.

But Sandro and Marco said that this line of thought was not common in Rome. And Romans are generally quite satisfied having the same jobs in the same place with the same people for most of their lives. And you know what? I found this to be a pleasing idea. These guys are who they are. They are doing what they do. And much of their definition of self was set. It's interesting to know exactly what you're going to get. Eliminates the guess work.

"So what kind of job is so great that you want to stay in it your whole life?" I looked at Marco, knowing his answer before he said anything. "Okay, so being a bodyguard to the

Pope might be the Holy Grail of security." I asked him who he likes better, the new Pope or the old Pope. (This was before the newer Pope, Francis, arrived on the scene.)

"I love both Popes. Pope Benedict is *very* intelligent." Then he looked off and said, "Pope John Paul had a *very* big heart." His eyes watered. "I miss my old friend." Sandro put his hand on his friend's shoulder in comfort and support.

Romans just whip out their emotions and throw them down on the table for you to admire alongside the antipasti, pasta, and strawberries.

Sandro works for the gas company. "I make sure the monuments light up so we can attract the tourist dollars." And with that, we left the restaurant and meandered to a perch overlooking the glowing Colosseum to admire his handiwork.

"What will you do now?" Sandro asked.

I hesitated. "I'd like to be an artist."

He smiled, put his arm around my shoulders, and gave me a squeeze. "I was hoping you would say that."

I told him about the painted letters of Percy Kelly and about my new little set of watercolors. He asked me for a paper and pen. I pulled out my journal. He wrote down his mailing address and handed the journal to Marco, who did the same.

"Send us painted letters," he said.

The next day, I sat by a fountain in Villa Borghese and began my first painted letter for Sandro. A few days later, after a stifling hot but fun adventure with my two favorite Romans, I recounted our time together in my second painted letter, this time for Marco.

Dear Sandro,

The fountains of Rome make all the noise of the city stop. I can sit next to a fountain, listen to the trickling water, and come back to myself. All the other sounds fade away so that I can only hear my thoughts and the soothing fountain. It's as if they've agreed—the fountain and my ears—to drown out everything else so we could all collect ourselves and our thoughts for the next leg of the journey. But sometimes the only word I hear is "stay."
  Janice

Dear Sandro,

The fountains of Rome make all the noise of the city stop. I can sit next to a fountain, listen to the trickling water, and come back to myself. All the other sounds fade away so that I can only hear my thoughts and the soothing fountain. It's as if they've agreed — the fountain and my ears — to drown out everything else so we could all collect ourselves and our thoughts for the next leg of the journey. But sometime the only word I hear is "stay."

Janice

Dear Marco,

There are many questions I have about the Italian language, like whether to add the "H" as shown above. My Google Search proved fruitless. My day at Villa (H)Adriana will always be remembered fondly for the beauty of the ruins, but more for the company. I laugh to recall standing in the shade and traipsing through the woods in search of the exit. And of course, the many photos I made you pose for along the way. I'm like a Japanese tourist with my camera. Thank you for a dreamy day among the ruins.

   Janice

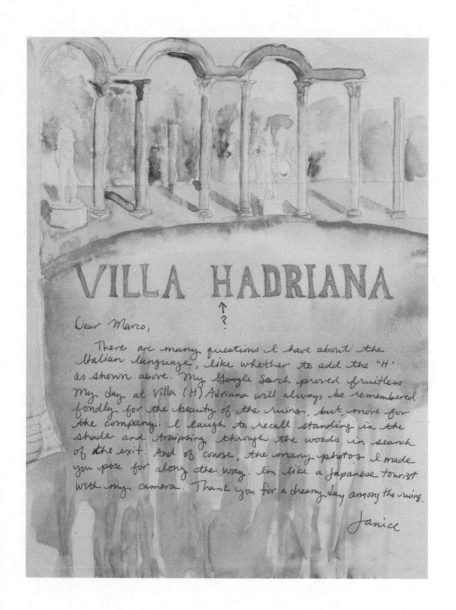

VILLA HADRIANA

↑
?

Dear Marco,

There are many questions I have about the Italian language, like whether to add the "H" as shown above. My Google Search proved fruitless. My day at Villa (H) Adriana will always be remembered fondly for the beauty of the ruins, but more for the company. I laugh to recall standing in the shade and traipsing through the woods in search of the exit. And of course, the many photos I made you pose for along the way. I'm like a Japanese tourist with my camera. Thank you for a dreamy day among the ruins.

Janice

15

Bridge of Sighs

In life, we must accept who is asking and accept who is not. There was no one asking me to stay in Rome, and I had the lovely Christophe asking me to return to Paris. So why didn't I just go back to Paris? I had been on the road for two months by this point. I was getting traveler fatigue and was missing my lovely butcher boyfriend. And yet, I kept on traveling. Why? Because though I had learned to say no back in LA to events and people that drained my energy and wallet, I had yet to learn when to say no to myself.

I had a full Italy itinerary. For a week after my paella dinner with my favorite Romans, I walked and walked and walked, stopping only to eat gelato and street pizza, paint, or write in my journal. I even took up doing the rosary, adding the activity to my long list of things to do each day. See this, see that. Do this, do that. Add an Italian language lesson, research cooking lessons, yet keep walking. I took a train to the Amalfi coast, but it wasn't the same without Áine by my side to toss eggs into the sea. I walked across Sorrento, over Positano, and when I reached the island of Capri and had the option to take the elevator or the stairs up to the top of the island, I took the stairs. When I was tired, I took the train to Florence and walked more. Up and down the Duomo (the cathedral of Santa Maria del Fiore), through the open-air sculpture gallery in Piazza della Signoria to see a replica of Michelangelo's David, then onto the Galleria dell'Accademia for a quick hello to the original. Walk, walk, walk. Click photos, keep walking.

By the time I reached Venice, I could do nothing but sigh from exhaustion. Luckily, I was in good company. The entire city of Venice seemed like it was sighing, as if it was also tired of holding itself together. With the coming and going of tides, the pastel buildings slowly rose and sank from the verdant watery grave. Boats puttered along the canals, schlepping everything from bananas and artichokes to grand pianos. Though San Marco Square was buzzing with tourists, beyond the square was a maze of vacant alleyways where no one ventured except a lost tourist. Trust me on this.

Even the gondola men seemed to only sing sad love songs. The city was fading like a masterpiece painting left in the sun too long. And when the sun went down and all the workers had taken the last water taxis out of the city, it was a gloomy and eerie ghost town.

It was all a bit depressing. Yet at the same time, beautiful. And definitely a nice place to get reflective.

One evening, I was walking along the canal at night. I was alone. I mean, really alone. I saw one couple walking hand-in-hand and no one else. On the one side of me was the canal with the quiet sound of boats buzzing by. On the other side of me was a hedge of jasmine. It was a warm night in June, and the jasmine fragrance filled the air. Venice was lovely, even in the lonely parts.

I stood on one of the many bridges and peered down to my reflection in the lapping water. The girl in the reflection looked different. Thinner from all the walking, despite all the eating. But she had a different kind of tired around her eyes. This time it wasn't from too much paperwork under fluorescent lights. It was the look of a girl who was tired of carrying her luggage.

I thought back to the day I cleaned out my underwear drawer

and to all those men whom my undies had represented. Why hadn't any of those relationships worked out? I saw now, as I gazed down at this girl in the water, back then I had become who they wanted me to be. If a guy was a granola-eating hippie, so was I. If he was a hipster beach bum, I had a beach cruiser at the ready. *Just let me lace up my Converse.* If he was a runner, I was a runner. If he was a hiker, I'd buy books on local hiking trails and suggest a few. I'd stash oranges and chocolate in my backpack to surprise him with a treat at the top of the hill. *Look at how amazing I am at hiking.*

I was also agonizingly relatable. If they were arguing a point, I'd give them even more arguments in defense of their own point so they would feel even more correct in their opinions. I was convincing them to like me just as I convinced people to buy what I was selling in the junk mail I created. I would do and be whatever they loved because what I loved was being loved. Being loved was paramount to my own inner beliefs, opinions, and preferences. I took their traits and copied them as my own. *Don't worry about who I am. Who do you want me to be?* Akemi was right. *You're a copywriter. That's who you are.* In junk mail and in life.

No, no. No.

I peered down at my reflection again, and something was wrong. I saw something that no longer belonged in my new life. I took off my apple pin and looked at it closely. I'd been carrying the dream of being a copywriter with me long after the dream faded. With one flick of my finger, I let it fall out of my hands and into the water, watching it sink into the murky waters of Venice. And with that, the last of my old wardrobe fell.

That girl peering back at me from the water was me, just me. The real me. Not the other versions I tried to be to win anyone over. I took a breath and exhaled. I forgave myself for my prior judgments of not being good enough to be just who I was. The truth was I was just doing the best I could with what I knew at the time. But now I knew better.

I thought I'd cry here on the bridge with all these insights pouring out of me. I used to cry every single day, usually about some boy, sometimes about pressure at work. There was always something to cry about. But now, I hadn't cried since that tiny two-minute episode when I said good-bye to Christophe at the airport in Paris. How unlike me. Or, perhaps, the crying version of me no longer existed. That was who I was before, not who I was on this bridge in Venice. Along the way, I replaced a bad habit of being upset with a good habit of being happy. Could it really be that simple?

Christophe was the only man I dated with whom I could not contort my own personality to create his fantasy girl, simply because I didn't have the language skills with which to do so. With Christophe, I had opinions, simple as they were. When he would ask if I wanted to go here or there, I would respond with *Oui* or *Non*. I used to respond with something like, "Well, if you'd like to. Are you sure? What do you want? If you want to go there, we will." All these words! All these agreeables. I was tired of talking, tired of trying, tired of the costumes.

Christophe was waiting for me in Paris. He had asked me return to Paris to stay with him "to see." Indeed. To see what I had been blind to for so long. Since I had left, he had called six times a day, a staggering amount by North American standards. I didn't know if he was psycho, paranoid, or in love. He was from Poland, so it was tough to tell. When I asked him about this, he replied that he simply wanted to pick up the charges for the calls so I wouldn't have to. He appeared to fall so head over heels in love with me that I didn't quite trust the strength of his affection, never having experienced it before. We were both steeped in the glorious two weeks of honeymooning in Paris. Was that real love or just a nice couple of weeks?

Since the message he had sent me upon my arrival in Rome,

I had told him I was thinking about returning but hadn't given him a solid yes. My thoughts went back to what Ben had said in London. "*What could happen? Happiness? Great. Ruin? You can handle that. Do you think you'll lose everything and become homeless? You already got rid of everything. You're already homeless.*"

There and then, I decided I would go back to Paris to be with Christophe. Freedom's just another word for nothing left to lose.

❧ 16 ❧

Unpacking in Paris

I arrived back in Paris on a warm evening at the end of June with considerably less baggage.

I was waiting at baggage claim at Paris Orly Airport when I spotted Christophe. He looked panicked, scouring the signs, looking for my flight number and me. When he saw me, he took a deep breath and grinned. The panic disappeared. My heart was pumping in my ears so loud that when we came together and kissed, I heard nothing. No blaring airport announcements, no hum of the crowd, no mesh of languages, no clacking high-heel shoes. The world was silent. We pulled out of our kiss and I choked my tears down.

"*Bonjour*, my darling."

"When did you learn the word *darling*?"

He winked and took my suitcase in one hand, my hand in the other, and we walked toward the train to Paris in relative silence.

We were never about words anyway.

Christophe's apartment was tiny, but he had completely transformed it to look startlingly similar to the citizenM hotel in Glasgow (had he remembered the photos I sent?). Everything had been painted, cleaned up, and cleared away to prepare for my arrival. Now here I was, in my own little citizenM room in the heart of Paris. He had even purchased matching robes, explaining that we should feel like we were on vacation all the time. And he had bought and assembled new furniture, including a wardrobe. (The French do not have closets. This mystifies me.)

He pointed to it, inviting me to unpack my suitcase. And I did. My tiny piles of shirts and pants each had their own wide shelves. I hung my few dresses. And I smiled as I set my small pile of undies, which had been purchased for his viewing pleasure, next to my T-shirts.

I collapsed next to him on the bed and he slowly peeled off the rest of my wardrobe. We made love by moonlight.

The next morning, he gave me all I ever really wanted after a night like that: coffee in bed and the login information for high-speed Internet access.

When you're on the road, Internet access is often sketchy, slow, nonexistent, or pricey. When I told him I would stay with him, I added that I would need high-speed Internet. He may have been the last man in the Western world to order in-home Internet.

Each morning of this first month together, he would get up, make coffee, and deliver it to me in bed. "*Bonjour*, my darling."

"*Bonjour, mon amour.*" We would kiss.

Over coffee, he would ask me what I would do during the day. I would tell him in simple French words. I would ask him what he would do. He would laugh and say the same, which was that he would go to work at the butcher shop up the street. Once he left, I would go back to bed. Eventually I would rise, make another coffee, and go online. I lived for the stockpile of emails that came in during the night from my friends in Canada and the United States. They wrote funny comments on my blog to keep in touch.

Christophe would come home at lunch. We would usually make sandwiches of fresh baguette (still warm from the *boulangerie* ovens), cheese, and meat. Afterward, we would have a sweet lovemaking session and a nap. He would tell me my body was "ideal," which was lovely to hear despite the awareness that his ideal was a Rodin sculpture while mine was closer to Lady Gaga. Afterward, he would head back to work.

On occasion, I would imagine myself packing my things right after he left. I imagined I would walk myself to the Métro, head to the airport, and leave all this behind. It would be so easy to go when one has so little to pack. Plus, after a year of dreaming of leaving and a long time of coming and going, it was hard to remember how to stay. But after time, these thoughts of a quick getaway faded. I wasn't going anywhere without Christophe.

Unless it was in Paris, of course. I walked a lot while he was at work. I walked to iron out the thoughts in my head. I walked to burn calories from all my culinary explorations.

At the end of the day, Christophe brought home meat from the butcher shop that I cooked for dinner. My vegan days were definitely over. So were my cardboard box days. We ate on plates.

I still wasn't fluent in French though. I studied French through podcasts, audio CDs, and an online language class. I was determined to be bilingual but couldn't quite bring myself to sign up for a physical class, still reeling from office desk trauma. The online class had badges I could earn and green check marks to encourage me along the way. I collected these like a good Girl Guide, hoping the collection would magically transform me into a more advanced version of myself. The Janice 2.0 that could speak French. But then I would turn on the TV to marvel once again at just how befuddled I was with the language. I hoped that one day I would know exactly what they were saying. But for a long time, it was all a picture show with some mysterious language thrown in to confuse me.

It all got very tiring, and I slept a lot during that first summer in Paris. In this life where I could be as active or as lazy as I wanted to be, it was easy to sit on the couch and tell myself I was just "coming down" from my fourteen years as a copywriter in advertising. While that may have been true in the months after I quit my job, it had been a long time since then.

The only job I had in Paris was blogging, and it didn't exactly qualify as a job. Except for the occasional donation I received, I wasn't making any money from it. I painted letters for my donators and mailed them off with a thank-you message.

I sat in Jardin du Luxembourg a lot too. One hot day, I brought along the watercolors. I sat in front of a fountain and fished out some water in a plastic cup I had brought for the occasion. I opened my journal and I began painting. And that's when Percy Kelly showed up.

Percy Kelly died in the 1990s, but as I painted, I could feel his voice in my head. It was my voice but with an edge, and it was instructing me as I painted.

"See this line here?" he whispered. "This is a good place to start. And here? Leave that white. That will be the splashing water later." He continued. "And don't worry about dripping paint. It's a fountain, ferchrissake." This guy definitely had a different tone than Mr. Miyagi. I listened and painted under the shade of a willow tree, then took out my pen and wrote.

Dear Áine,

Paris does something to a person. It unleashes the pent-up romantic. Even if you're not the touchy-feely type, you find yourself begging to hold hands and grope the nearest person as you walk over a bridge just so you can say later that you did it and wasn't that marvelous. What was his name? Does it matter?

You gasp at statues, staring at their curves, forming crushes. Even all the Jesuses in all the churches get you flustered. Remember Rome? Those abs. The hero. I shake my head at the inappropriate thoughts, but still keep staring.

In my wanderings, I came across this fountain in Jardin du Luxembourg. When I first came upon this couple, I came undone. I hadn't yet started dating Christophe. Despite my best efforts to embrace being alone, what I really wanted was to be the girl on the rock in the arms of an adoring man. A quiet voice from deep within eeked out, "Yes, please."

A few days later, Christophe kissed me and we began our little Paris love affair. Sometimes we sit next to this fountain together and listen to the trickle of water that makes all the noise of the city fade away. Afterward, if we don't know what to say or how to say it, we meander over to the Seine and walk over one of the bridges hand-in-hand so I can say later, "Wasn't that marvelous?!"

Janice

Dear Áine,

Paris does something to a person. It unleashes the pent-up romantic. Even if you're not the touchy-feely type, you find yourself begging to hold hands and grope the nearest person as you walk over a bridge just so you can say later that you did it and wasn't that marvelous. What was his name? Does it matter?

You gasp at statues, staring at their curves, forming crushes. Even all the Jesuses in all the churches get you flustered. Remember Rome? Those abs. The hero. I shake my head at the inappropriate thoughts, but still keep staring.

In my wanderings, I came across this fountain in Jardin du Luxembourg. When I first came upon this couple, I came undone. I hadn't yet started dating Christophe. Despite my best efforts to embrace being alone, what I really wanted was to be the girl on the rock in the arms of an adoring man. A quiet voice within from deep within eeked out. "Yes, please."

A few days later, Christophe kissed me and we began our little Paris love affair. Sometimes we sit next to this fountain together and listen to the trickle of water that makes all the noise of the city fade away. Afterward, if we don't know what to say or how to say it, we meander over to the Seine and walk over one of the bridges hand-in-hand so I can say later, "Wasn't that marvelous?!"

♡ Janice

17

The Paris Letter Project

A few days later, after I had I stopped by the butcher shop and puckered up for a *petit bisou* with Christophe, I zigzagged my way to Les Deux Magots on boulevard Saint-Germain. This is the famous café where Simone de Beauvoir sipped legal addictive stimulants while concocting big ideas that would later win her worldwide acclaim. This café serves American-style coffee and fresh-baked croissants, and boasts a fantastic view of the street. A perfect place to be alone among others. De Beauvoir knew what she was doing.

I sat inside, away from the hustle-bustle of the *terrasse*. Come summer, the cafés of Paris fold back their outer walls so that wherever you sit, inside or out, you can soak in the warm summer breeze. I pulled out my journal. By now, I had been writing in my journal for a year and a half, and it became my home base. The one constant foreground when all my backgrounds shifted. The place where I could figure out the next steps.

Now the next step wouldn't be figuring out which city to visit, but what I could do with myself from one place. The time had come when I had to revisit my reserve. The bank account had taken a plunge with all my travels, and so did a few of my stocks. It was time to figure out how to replenish the buffer so it would always be ahead of me and I would never be forced back into a draining job of time sheets and vacation accrual.

But what could I do to make cash?

I would consult my journal, just as I had done from the beginning. I would write my way to the answer, at times with help from Mr. Miyagi. I opened my journal, and my letter to Áine slipped out. As I looked it over, I thought that I'd rather create another painted letter than sit writing through ideas to make money to boost my account.

And of course, that was the answer.

It was always the letter. Painted letters from Paris to delight Áine, who was busy carving out her career, this time in Toronto. Painted letters to my friends in Rome to thank them for a lovely holiday and supporting my little artistic dreams from that night sitting outside the Colosseum. Painted letters for anyone who donated on my blog. A grateful thank-you from the road for their support. Would other people want painted letters from Paris too?

But these letters would take time. I couldn't create a new letter for every person who wanted one. I'd end up back where I started: too much work, too little time.

Akemi's voice came into my head. *You're a copywriter. That's who you are.*

Copy. Writer. Copy writing.

Copy the letter. Personalize each copy.

Of course. When I wrote junk mail letters, I would start them all with "Dear FName." The FName stood for First Name and was the code that told the computer to replace each FName with the first name of the recipient of the letter. I would do the same with my painted letters, but instead of using a computer, I would write in the name with a pen. It wouldn't be an original letter for each person, but if I did it this way, the whole process would be more time-effective for me and more affordable for a subscriber. I thought back to my original equation of $100 a day. Would I rather make $100 from creating one painted letter for one person? Or would I rather get $5 from twenty people for a copied letter? What would I pay for a painted letter? I would pay $5 for a copy rather than $100 for the original, especially if I were engaged in some escape artistry and would need those other $95 to meet my financial goals.

So that's what I would do. I would create a painted letter, copy it, personalize each copy, and mail them off to people who love fun mail.

I consult the Percy Kelly in my mind.

"Go for it. What could happen? I'll help when you get stuck."

I tossed a few coins on the table and nearly ran home.

My first official painted letter was copied, personalized, and mailed to a dozen friends with notes saying I would send them a letter like this each month for a year. I committed to a year of letters so I wouldn't chicken out. I had to be accountable to someone, just as I was with my blog in 2010 when I had vowed to write in my journal every day for a year. With people reading, I was more likely to stick to the plan.

I listed the product on Etsy as a subscription service. For twelve months, people would receive a painted letter from me. I advertised my new service on the usual social media streams and waited for orders.

A few days later, I woke to Christophe delivering a coffee to bed. We sat in bed and sipped. I explained the concept to him. He nodded. "It's for joy." He got it.

"*Oui*. Mail for joy."

Halfway through the cup, he started to get ready for his workday, which couldn't happen soon enough because I was already reaching for my phone to check to see if I had any orders.

Which I did!!!! Blessings ahoy!

I had about a dozen orders. They were all from friends, but still, actual orders.

When he left for work, he said, "Go back to sleep. It's early." I nodded. But when the front door closed, I leapt out of bed, slipped into my yoga pants, and began fulfilling orders. Envelopes! Printouts! Ink! Stamps! Heaven!

Later, I walked up the street with these little beauties and stopped at the butcher shop for another smooch with Christophe, grateful that it was a pleasure for him to give me the large amount of kisses I required. He saw my handful of envelopes and smiled. I skipped/ran to the post office and sent these little envelopes of bliss on their merry way.

One might think, *Isn't this STILL a lot like Direct Mail, the career I left all dramatic-like?* I admit, I was actually creating mail that goes directly to a person, which may seem a lot like direct mail. But with this Paris Letter service, I was sending mail to people who actually wanted it. People who paid for it. People who welcomed it.

I imagined they would come home from a long day at work, grab the mail, see the usual junk mail, and sigh. "Not this crap again." But inside that little pile of envelopes was a sweet little letter from Paris. "Ah, it's here." Eyes narrowing, grins forming.

Orders trickled in at a constant rate. Enough to keep me busy and with enough cash so I didn't have to tap into the reserve too often. People I didn't even know started subscribing. When I would tell Christophe about new orders, he would say, "You know these people?" and I would exclaim joyfully, "NO! They are all strangers. Isn't that wonderful!"

As I addressed the envelopes over the next few months, I wondered about the receivers. How was Janet from Peculiar, Missouri, doing? And Ronda who lived on Pughs Store Road. I'd love to ask her if there still is, or ever was, an actual store named after a Pughs. If so, was Pughs the store owner or an important historical figure of the town? How was Susan in Lucknow doing these days? How about Liz on the Lake Road who lived in Driftwood Point. Or Leila in Las Vegas who sold a few things on eBay to pay for her letters. Then there was Miss Love who lives on Flowery Branch Road. I bet she loved writing her address. When I was a kid, I grew up at RR#1, Clear Creek, Ontario, Canada. The RR stands for rural route and wasn't nearly as interesting as the address for Mrs. Golden, who lived on Sugar Creek Trail. Such lovely addresses from places I've never been. I felt like I was traveling to these distant lands without leaving my base in Paris.

I thought of the names of my subscribers, too, as I would address their letters. How their parents usually did a pretty good job naming them. I would admire how the double Ls in Sally's first name matched the double Ls in her last name. How Joshua and Jones was a nice pair. There were a lot of Jennifers, Jennys, Jens, and Jenns. And Lindas, Lynnes, and Lynns. The Catherines, Katherines, Kathleens, Cathys, Kathys, and Kates. They all had to be kept straight. And then there were the zip codes and the street names. Dreamy street names introduced themselves with every order: Forest Lake Drive, Pear Tree Lane, Garland Street, Chestnut Street, Mistletoe Way, Mossy Creek Court, Letterman Way, and my favorite, Yellow Brick Drive.

It was all juicy fun until the lame subscribers arrived, who, on occasion, were expecting the original painting rather than a personalized copy of the original painting. As if I would spend days painting a scene of Paris just to sell them for less than the cost of a pit stop at Starbucks. They were just like old clients who wanted more, more, more for less. I tried to treat these people like I did when faced with dog poop on the sidewalks in Paris. A glance out of the periphery of my vision, a smooth sidestep, and an erasing of the moment from my mind.

Dear Áine,

It's raining in Paris today. Not all day, just when I gear up to go. The clouds seem to know when I put on my coat, and they take it as a cue to downpour. So while I wait for the latest downpour to subside, I'm writing this letter to you and sipping coffee.

My haste to get outside is based on an exciting call I received after lunch. The book I ordered has arrived at the local English bookstore. There is something poetic about a good old-fashioned bookstore. I used to have Amazon deliver books to my door. I've always had a love for mail and these days, I'll be the first to brag about the convenience and pleasure of e-books. The instant access to English books in a French-speaking land is a magical delight. But there is magic in traditional bookstores too. It's a magic you can feel in the air. The smell of aging paper, of ink, and of people. And in Paris, some of those people were Hemingway and Fitzgerald.

The rain has subsided for now. The clouds are likely waiting for me to lace up my shoes. Walking in the rain in Paris isn't so bad. The sound of the rain hitting my umbrella is pleasant, and the light from the lampposts glistens on the sidewalk.

Janice

Dear Áine,

It's raining in Paris today. Not all day, just when I gear up to go. The clouds seem to know when I put on my coat, and they take it as a cue to downpour. So while I wait for the latest downpour to subside, I'm writing this letter to you and sipping coffee.

My haste to get outside is based on an exciting call I received after lunch. The book I ordered has arrived at the local English bookstore. There is something poetic about a good old-fashioned bookstore. I used to have Amazon deliver books to my door. I've always had a love for mail. And these days, I'll be the first to brag about the convenience and pleasure of e-books. The instant access to English books in a French-speaking land is a magical delight. But there is magic in traditional bookstores too. It's a magic you can feel in the air. The smell of aging paper, of ink, and of people. And in Paris, some of those people were Hemingway and Fitzgerald.

The rain has subsided for now. The clouds are likely waiting for me to lace up my shoes. Walking in the rain in Paris isn't so bad. The sound of the rain hitting my umbrella is pleasant, and the light from the lampposts glistens on the sidewalk.

Janice

18

Our First Fight

Christophe continued to shower me with affection: bringing me coffee, holding my hand, taking the occasional mouse-traps out to *finish the job*. (Now I know why *Ratatouille* was set in Paris.) Everything was perfect.

Until I changed things.

When I first moved in and saw that Christophe had repainted and made the house pretty, I was delighted with all of it. However, the carpet in the bedroom horrified me. We're talking 1985 carpet that they install in schools. So I went ahead and laid a floor on top of the carpet. By. My. Self.

Why?

Because Christophe thought the floor was just fine as it was. When I asked him about changing the floor, he explained, quite reasonably, that he didn't own the place and a new floor crossed the line of home improvements that he could do. I had already duct-taped over holes along the floorboards and wondered if anyone would cross those lines.

I had never actually installed a floor before, but my dad is a flooring guy, and when I was a kid, I picked up a lot watching him. Still, I was a little scared to start. Not only because I had just moved in with a guy and he said no. But the first time doing anything new tends to bring up plenty of fears of not being talented enough, smart enough, or even just physically strong enough. To combat said fears, I did two things:

I told a few friends I was doing it. They did a wonderful job in giving me the permission I wanted to give myself to lay that floor.

Remembering my twenty-minute trick from when I cleared out my apartment back in California, I set my alarm. I told myself I only had to do it for twenty minutes and then I could rest and move on to something else. With the support of friends behind me and twenty minutes ahead of me, I began. After the first twenty minutes, I had a few planks down. They were looking pretty good, so I put another twenty minutes on the clock and another few planks down. Four hours later (including another trip to the hardware store because I hadn't measured correctly), I was done and the bedroom was worthy of being featured in a design magazine. The job was akin to putting together a big jigsaw puzzle or massive sticker collection. I had a pile of dull blades from my cutting knife, bruises up and down my arms, and a smile of satisfaction on my face.

Three cheers for me!

I also had half a pack of the planks left over, so I covered the old shelf in the bathroom, and my original smile of satisfaction turned into beams of pride.

Then Christophe came home.

There are those moments at the beginning of a relationship when you test each other. I suppose this entire exercise was a test to see what he was like when triggered. He came in the house, looked at the floor, looked at me. I beamed. "I did it myself!" He said nothing. Instead, he suggested we go to the grocery store to get food for dinner. And in that little jaunt up the street, he was silent, a different silence than the usual language barrier. He was probably wondering, *Is this how she is?* And I was wondering the same about him. *Is he a silent-treatment guy?*

Somewhere between the apples and oranges, he turned to me. "Why did you change the floor after I said no?"

"Because you said no, and I wanted to do it anyway. It makes me happy, and I like to be happy."

Talking to someone in another language makes you simply cut to the chase. You just don't know enough words to pussy-foot around a situation.

"It makes you happy?"

"Yes." Hands on hips. "Even if it makes you mad."

He laughed. I laughed. He likely wondered what he was getting into by dating me. Later he admitted that, though he retained his opinion that it looked fine before, he noticed that my added joviality around the house made me sexier.

"Great," I said. "Can we get shower doors now?"

He sighed. I decided not to push it. We came home, and he played love songs on the guitar while I made pasta.

In Paris, insistence on beauty has seeped into the culture so much that Parisians become offended by having to look at something that isn't lovely. It's probably why everyone gets dolled up to run across the street for two minutes to grab a *brioche*. Why yoga pants are only for yoga or lounging around alone at home. Why the green garbage trucks patrol the city like an occupying army. Or why, when you're just out grabbing a few groceries to feed your family, you expect to be treated to a beautiful food display to feed your soul.

Or why you'll change the bedroom floor anyway.

Dear Áine,

History is everything and everywhere in Paris. You walk on it, sit on it, and live with it every day.

Train stations, streets, and cafés are named after famous people or events, and everyone seems to know why. Everyone knows where Hemingway sipped cocktails (where didn't he?), that Edith Piaf sang for cents on the streets of Pigalle, and that George-Eugène Haussman carved Paris into the grand city it is today. He gave himself the title of Baron even though technically he was merely a Monsieur. He tore down and rebuilt Paris under the rule of Napoleon III, who gave himself a title too — Emperor of France. Napoleon III is not to be confused with Napoleon I who actually WAS the Emperor of France.

Dear Áine,

History is everything and everywhere in Paris. You walk on it, sit on it, and live with it every day. Train stations, streets, and cafés are named after famous people or events, and everyone seems to know why. Everyone knows where Hemingway sipped cocktails (where didn't he?), that Edith Piaf sang for cents on the streets of Pigalle, and that George-Eugène Haussman carved Paris into the grand city it is today. He gave himself the title of Baron even though technically he was merely a Monsieur. He tore down and rebuilt Paris under the rule of Napoleon III, who gave himself a title too—Emperor of France. Napoleon III is not to be confused with Napoleon I who actually WAS the Emperor of France.

"Baron" Haussman built bridges, bourgeois apartments, and grand boulevards. These streets "happened" to be wide enough for the government to flex its military muscle on the people. A cannonball, after all, can't make a sharp right in a medieval town.

It all worked out in the end—more or less—and these days, come Bastille Day, crowds gather to cheer the tanks, trucks, and soldiers as they strut their stuff in the parade.

A few streets escaped Haussman's ambitious plans—my street included, which makes my apartment older than any building across the Atlantic. People have been making meals, making babies, washing, and sleeping in my petit palace for centuries. And though I try not to think about it, they've likely died here too. People who may have even had a hand in building up the new city around them.

I don't sense ghosts though. They are probably out enjoying the warm weather. I think I'll do the same right after I head to the post office to send off this letter. The flowers are in bloom, and a few trees are wearing chestnuts like earrings. It's a new day in Paris. History in the making.

Au revoir!
Empress Janice

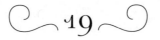

How Would You Like Your Eggs?

Unfertilized, please.

It was August. A few months into my life with Paris. I was in bed and hoping for menstrual cramps. It was day 34 and my period usually arrives on day 28.

Pregnancy, or the possibility thereof, really puts into perspective how much love exists between two people.

I would have been relieved at the sight of blood. I was definitely falling in love with Christophe, but it felt too soon. I was still seeing about us. The two of us.

Years ago, I dated a man who wanted to have a baby with me. At the first opportunity, I broke it off, my fallopian tubes nearly tying themselves in knots in order to say, "No, this guy's swimmers are not going to mingle with these eggs."

Christophe and I had been careful and consistent in our lovemaking, but our numerous rolls in the hay during our first few months together weren't putting the odds in our favor. A few sperm slipping by multiplied by the daily conjugality? Only abstinence is 100 percent.

I spent the morning drifting off into the pregnancy scenario. I was in my mid-thirties. I was not sixteen. I was an adult. We would deal. And though it was great that the option for termination exists, it was not an option for me anymore. I was with a man who could be a good husband and good father. The only hesitation was that it was too soon. We were fresh. We were new.

He came home for lunch with couscous and eggs of some sort of "delicacy." They were boiled eggs wrapped in ham and steeped in a salty, brown gelatin. Why do the French always dress food like it's going to a black-tie event? They were eggs. This was lunch at home. Why all the fuss? Let them be. But they were here, and they were cold. It was hot in Paris that day. This was no time to turn on the stove. No reason to turn up the heat.

"Do you think we should get a pregnancy test?" I asked, wondering if he'd say, "No, don't worry about it," or "Yes, let's find out now."

"You want?" he replied, which is also what he said when he thought I was suitably warmed up for intercourse.

"No, forget it. I'm afraid taking the test will make me pregnant."

He laughed. I laughed nervously. I wasn't kidding.

He grabbed his house key, saying he'd be back in five minutes. In that five minutes, I cried and prayed. *Please God, let me not be pregnant.*

The eggs were left on the plate untouched.

When he returned, I unwrapped the home pregnancy test. I asked if he had ever done one of these before. He had not. Nor had I.

The instructions were in French. He read the French while I searched for the English instructions online. We agreed to collect the urine in a cup, soak the stick for twenty seconds, then wait the interminable three minutes for the results. We used a stopwatch.

We kissed inside the three minutes and agreed that whatever happened would be good. I swear the test was designed for a three-minute wait so that couples would come to some sort of definition of where they stood as a couple: peace accord, matrimony, or an amicable parting of the ways.

A minute and a half in and I glanced at the instructions that were printed in French. I was preparing for *Not pregnant* or *Pregnant*, but I realized that I needed to look for the *Pas* in front of *enceinte*.

Pas pas pas pas pas pas, please let there be a *pas*.

Our eyes darted between the stopwatch and the screen. Minute three arrived.

Pas enceinte.

I was relieved. He kissed me.

Our eggs were waiting. We sat down to lunch.

In a split second, his true feelings showed on his face. He was devastated. I started to cry.

"Maybe in a year?" he asked.

"Just not now," I responded.

"Okay."

I swallowed hard on my egg. We finished lunch.

"Coffee?" I asked.

"You want?" he said.

I nodded.

Later, I sat in the park and watched children play. I mulled over the episode from lunch. What was so wrong with pregnancy? Every person at this park was the result of that moment when the test read positive. When there was no *pas* in front of the *enceinte*.

There was a young mother playing on the equipment with her child. She had bucked up. What's my problem?

People have children all the time, and with less than what Christophe and I had. We had much love and kindness for each other. And though he didn't know it, I had a decent portfolio that happily grew greener the more I painted my little letters. Maybe he had one too. Maybe we were rich and we didn't know it.

He came home after work, and I announced that my period was still MIA. He rubbed my belly, and I quipped, "That lump is just fat. Too much cheese." He laughed and told me he loved my lump. I was wearing a sundress. I took his sweatshirt off a hook, rolled it in a ball, and put it up my dress, mimicking a big pregnant belly.

"*Bonne. Tu es très belle*," he remarked and took a photo with his phone.

I stared at the bump. This isn't so bad, I thought. I remembered the young mother in the park. Was her pregnancy the result of planning? Or was her test without the *Pas* the result of a careful but consistent month of lovemaking?

I guess it depends on how lucky you are.

Christophe and I didn't make love that night. We said our *I love yous* and our *je t'aimes*. I tried to say I loved him in Polish. He advised me to stick to learning French for now. I stared at the ceiling and gave myopic attention to the slightest movement in my belly. Was it dinner working its way through? Or was something else working itself out?

Dear Áine,

A cemetery may seem like an odd place to come across a love story, but they say these types of things come along when you least expect them. After finding all the notable celebrities at Père Lachaise Cemetery—Oscar Wilde, Jim Morrison, and Edith Piaf to name a few—I came across an old lady carrying a heavy load. Normally, I don't stop to talk to strangers in Paris because they'll likely talk back in French and I'm still soaking up the words from my textbook, but this frail-looking creature looked like she could have used an extra hand, so I asked if I could help.

She nodded. "It's water," she explained. "I fill up the bottles at the main gate." Strangely, I understood her even though she spoke French. I asked her the universal traveler question, "Where are you from?" She told me she was from Poland, which explains why I understood her. I told her about Christophe, who is also from Poland but speaks to me in French. By now, I can't quite grasp the French language with a French accent, but I can understand some of it when spoken with a Polish accent.

As we walked through the cemetery, she told me that she and her husband left Poland during the war. "Everything was gone," she said. "Gone." They started again in Paris and had a good life. It wasn't always easy, "But we always had love, and that meant we had more than most."

She stopped, and we set down the water. She looked over to a grave. "He died last year," she said. In front of his grave was a lush flower garden. She bent down to pull a few weeds. "We lived in a small apartment nearby," she said. "He always wanted to give me a garden." I told her I was sorry for her loss. "Don't be, dear," she said. "I loved him enough to want him to go first. I was always better at handling the difficulties." She smiled wide. "He was better at the lighter side of life. He may be gone but not everything is gone. He left me with enough good memories to see me through until it's my time."

She straightened up, put her hands on her hips, and said, "Now, you're learning French. It's all about the verbs. Learn your verbs." We spoke further about this and that and soon it was time for me to continue on. As I turned to leave, she said, "Don't be sad for me, dear. This is how it should be. Though it may not seem like it, this is a happy ending to a long love story. It's what we all hope for. Thank you for helping me carry my load."

I realized later that I didn't catch her name. Whenever I return to the cemetery, I stop by his grave. I check on the flowers and pull a few weeds. For a long time, the flowers bloomed beautifully, until one day I returned to find a garden of stems and withered leaves. It was then when I found out that her name was Rose.

Janice

Dear Áine,

A cemetery may seem like an odd place to come across a love story, but they say these types of things come along when you least expect them. After finding all the notable celebrities at Père Lachaise Cemetery—Oscar Wilde, Jim Morrison and Edith Piaf to name a few—I came across an old lady carrying a heavy load.

Normally, I don't stop to talk to strangers in Paris because they'll likely talk back in French and I'm still sorting up the words from my text book, but this frail-looking creature looked like she could have used an extra hand, so I asked if I could help. She nodded.

"It's water," she explained. "I filled up bottles at the main gate." Strangely, I understood her even though she spoke French. I asked her the universal traveler question, "Where are you from?" She told me she was from Poland, which explains why I understood her. I told her about Christophe, who is also from Poland but speaks to me in French. By now, I can't quite grasp the French language with a French accent, but I can understand some of it when spoken with a Polish accent.

20

Rosé-Colored Glasses of Summer

The next day, my period arrived and I resumed my long walks across the city.

Summer in Paris was warm breezes, open-toed sandals, and gallons of pink wine. Flowers were nearly falling over themselves, hanging out windows, their petals lapping up the sunshine they hadn't tasted for months. Ladies were sashaying up the street and down through the Métro in brightly colored summer frocks. I saw many polka-dot undies wedged into some jiggling bums. Those ladies must not have realized how transparent their dresses really were, or they forgot to wear their slips, or they were French and that's how they rolled.

And then there was rosé wine.

Rosé is a refreshing young wine with hints of floral and grapefruit. And it's light as lace. You'd expect to see a few young girls sitting on patios drinking this blushing bride of wines. Rosé, before I knew better, was what people who don't drink wine slurped at weddings. I considered it wine-lite. It was sweet, cold, and…did I mention sweet? And after a few sips, there was a sense that this grape Kool-Aid was a bit…off.

In the United States and Canada, wine lovers scoff at the stuff. You're having white Zinfandel?! But here on the streets of Paris? Rosé was an honored beverage, a perfect combination of the reds of a cold winter and the refreshing whites of a hot summer. And

Parisians were clip-clopping in their shiny open-toed sandals to the nearest bar to partake in this refreshing pleasure. It became so popular in France that in 2008, it surpassed white wine sales. This was a big deal. The French aren't into change. At all. But they seem tickled by this pink potion.

Even big burly men with bellies out to *here* maneuvered themselves into sunny seats on crowded patios to sip dainty glasses of rosé while conversing about the president, women, the economy, and that whole mess. *Je crois* this and *je crois* that. "I believe" everyone had a different opinion on everything in the Eurozone, but we all agreed that rosé was where it was at when it came to summoning sunshine.

Now that I was going to be in Paris for the foreseeable future, I had to get busy finding friends to sit with me on patios and sip rosé. As Sandro mentioned in Rome, I had to find people with whom I could eat, drink, and laugh. Since returning from Italy, I had only been approached by men, or rather, whispered to by men in the street. I never caught what they said as they walked by so I ignored them, pretending I didn't hear. Max, the English-speaking bartender at Christophe's bar, informed me that they were whispering, "Adventure?"

"Does that actually work?" I asked, wide-eyed in my inno-cence. "Is that a thing?"

He shrugged. I was aware that men protect me from some aspects of their nature. I suspected Max was doing this with me now. Perhaps it was best not to know.

I wasn't really sure what to do about the friend thing. It wasn't my skill set. Now don't get the wrong idea. I actually do have friends. How they appeared in my life is a bit of a mystery to me, but it probably included a few nervous laughs and sweat on my part, and some extroverted efforts on their parts.

I thought back to a time in Canada when I stopped off at a playground with my niece. After fifteen minutes of scoping, she returned, hands on hips. "Well, I haven't met a new friend yet."

The playground didn't have many children due to inclement weather, so the pickin's were slim, but she was still confident that she'd meet a new friend to play with shortly.

I watched her approach other children. She seemed slightly shy, then she said anything she could to start up a conversation. If a kid fell, she would help him up. If another kid had a shovel, she offered to help make a sand castle—anything to get the party started. Soon they would be off and running as if they'd known each other all along.

When I was a little girl, playgrounds terrified me. I didn't know how to make friends or know what to say when children approached me. The whole playground friend-making affair was FAIL, FAIL, FAIL, time and time again. I usually ended up lagging behind my sister and her friends, or I played on the slide or swing, both of which are solitary games by nature. As long as I stayed on the slide or the swing, it was okay that I was alone.

My niece amazed me in her friend-making ability. I found myself studying her for tips. How did she approach other children so she didn't appear weird? How did the other children respond? How was she not afraid?

Watching my niece make her moves at the playground got me thinking that it's always good to have more friends, especially if Sandro was right and friends are the secret to happiness.

Christophe thought the same. While I was gallivanting around Italy, he was recruiting English-speaking girls whom he could set up with me if I decided to come back to Paris.

Melanie was in the lead. He asked for her number and explained that his girlfriend was Canadian and could use a friend. A blind date. Horrifying! But Melanie agreed because Christophe was nice and she liked his chicken. Plus, she hadn't been here too long herself, and it was always good to make new friends.

He came home one evening, handed me her number, and told me to call her. Agonizing! He said he was running out for five minutes to go pick up cigarettes. "Call her before I get back." So I did and I was so nervous that I would have rather just left Paris altogether because *What if I hated her?* Or worse, *What if she hated me?*

But I called because justdoitFAST. So I did it fast. And she agreed to meet me for a glass of wine. When Christophe arrived home, he and I traipsed up the street hand-in-hand but with me lagging behind. I was so scared that I actually thought that maybe the whole idea of leaving Los Angeles was a mistake and I would have been better off hanging out with the old crew.

Melanie walked up to us, introduced herself. Christophe skedaddled.

I opened the conversation with questions about how to get things done in Paris. She had been here two years and had the answers to my most burning questions: Where do you find pillows and clothes hangers? What is the Schengen Area all about? Should I be getting a Navigo pass? How does the Vélib' bike system work?

She knew all the answers, except for the question about the Vélib', which we could figure out together. After our rendezvous, I walked back to the bar down the street where Christophe was sitting with his friends.

"*Ça va?*" he asked. I told him she was nice and that we had arranged to go to a Meetup group together in a few days. "*Bon.*" And then he added his best Bob Marley, "Everything…is gonna be all right." He often spoke to me in lyrics. It was good that I knew so many songs.

Why do people go to Meetup groups? I question motivations. In the purest form, it's to meet nice people, to find new friends, to hear their stories. There is also, I suspect, an underlying desire to ward off bouts of loneliness, which require constant monitoring when one is an expat in a new country. And then there is the courting of ladies.

The Meetup group can be tough. A bunch of strangers

meeting up to chitchat. It's like online dating but odder, somehow. I think it has something to do with Meetup groups having a built-in curiosity about motivations.

Melanie and I went to an expat Meetup group that focused on wine tasting. "Go with your strengths," she said. When we walked in, we were greeted by the organizer who asked a few questions. "Oh, you're Canadian? How wonderful. There is a British gentleman you must meet." And he ushered us over to Simon, a tall, dapper fellow who was reading wine labels. Soon the organizer returned with Carole, a short brown-haired beauty with Snow White skin and red lips. She was Parisian but had lived in London for many years and was therefore expat in nature. I was enamored by her immediately. Though 100 percent bilingual, she began talking in yet another language: the language of wines. She led me around to various bottles and explained a little about the regions as we sipped along. Simon and Melanie also followed her lead, and our little Brit-esque group began to take form. At the end of the night when it was time to say farewell, I stood there nervously, hoping Carole and Simon would ask for my number. I had never asked for anyone's number before. And this Meetup group thing was beyond my scope of knowledge.

"If you come to this Meetup group again, can you let me know?" she asked.

"Sure!" I beamed and readily handed over my digits. Success!

"Let me know too," said Simon. More digits were exchanged.

When I arrived home, Christophe looked up from playing guitar. "*Ça va?*"

"*Ça va très bien!*" I told him I made two friends and one girl who asked for my number was from Paris. A native.

"*Fantastique*, my darling."

I had forgotten my cardigan at the wine bar and sent a message to my little group, asking if anyone had picked it up. Simon was the last to leave and saw the cardigan. Not knowing it was

mine, he handed it in to the girl behind the bar. The next day, I
had Melanie call (I couldn't quite master French on the phone).
The girl on the other end said there was no sign of any cardigan,
but I knew it was there somewhere, so the next day I traipsed
off to the bar to look for myself. When I walked in, I saw my
cardigan immediately. On the girl. She was wearing it. Oh dear,
I thought. Now I have to deal with this situation in French! I
approached her and talked to her eyebrows, not wanting to
look down at what was clearly my cardigan. I asked her if she
had seen my cardigan and that a friend had left it behind the
bar for me. She nodded and scurried to the back, coming out
a minute later with the cardigan in her hand. Warm. I smiled,
grabbed it, and did my own scurrying out the door. I nearly ran
to the Métro, feeling like I had stolen back my own cardigan.

Sharing my cardigan story would be a good excuse to get
together with my new friends. We started meeting all over Paris
for brunches, searching for the best Bloody Mary. We found
it at a New York restaurant called Joe Allen. Not surprising,
as the French aren't masters of brunch. Leave that to the New
Yorkers. Later, we went in search for the best *apéro*, the cocktail
hour after work and before dinner. We found it at Tourn'Bride
on 104 rue Mouffetard. Eventually, we graduated to the search
for the best wine bar. Simon found a little wine bar that offered
an impressive wine list and served delicious tapas. It was called
5e Cru at 7 rue du Cardinal-Lemoine, and this cozy little bar
soon became our place. The walls were lined with wines you
choose yourself, the quiche was the best I've had in my life,
and the long tables were lit with candles dripping down from
empty wine bottles. Soon our little group of four grew. Melanie
brought another friend, who brought another and another.
Before long, I was sipping wine and sharing in the delights of
daily life in Paris in cafés and bistros all over the city with a
lovely little collection of friends with whom I could eat, drink,
and laugh. Sandro would be so proud.

Dear Áine,

For my first two months in Paris, I was like Goldilocks, traipsing all over the city in search of the best café—a place I could call my own. One café would have a cozy atmosphere but terrible coffee. Another would have great coffee but terrible food. Then I came upon the café that was just right. It had it all—great coffee, cozy atmosphere, and traditional French cuisine. Plus, its location on the pedestrian-friendly rue Mouffetard makes it the perfect perch for people-watching.

Being here makes me feel like I'm in a timeless Paris—the version you see on all those postcards. People still sit and write letters, read the paper, and catch up on the latest gossip. I often linger here with my journal—sipping, dreaming, and listening to French words flutter by on the breeze. I plan on putting in plenty of time here, and at the end of my days, I'll likely haunt it ever after.

We all must find our place in this world. Here in Paris, I believe I've found mine.

À bientôt!
Janice

Dear Fine,

For my first two months in Paris, I was like Goldilocks, traipsing all over the city in search of the best café A place I could call my own. One café would have a cozy atmosphere but terrible coffee. Another would have great coffee but terrible food. Then I came upon the café that was just right. It had it all — great coffee, cozy atmosphere and delicious traditional French cuisine. Plus, its location on the pedestrian-friendly rue Mouffetard makes it the perfect perch for people watching. Being here makes me feel like I'm in a timeless Paris — the version you see on all those postcards. People still sit and write letters, read the papers, and catch up on the latest gossip. I often linger here with my journal — sipping, dreaming and listening to French words flutter by on the breeze. I plan on putting in plenty of time here, and at the end of my days, I'll likely haunt it ever after. We all must find our place in this world. Here in Paris, I believe I've found mine.

À bientôt!

Janice

21

Franglish

When I told people I was dating someone who didn't speak English, they said, quite reasonably, "But how do you COMMUNICATE?" and they drew out the word "communicate" as if I don't know what the word meant.

I usually said we didn't talk. Then I winked.

But it was a valid question. English is Christophe's fifth language, and with such a well-developed language brain, whatever words he picked up seemed to stick in his head. Conversely, the French words I picked up in one ear went out the other and back again like a pendulum until eventually they settled somewhere inside my noggin. Most of his English education came from song lyrics, which he continued to incorporate into our conversations. When I made a delicious meal, he informed me in song, "You are my sunshine, my only sunshine." And eventually he sang, "*Je m'en irai poser tes portraits à tous les plafonds de tous les palais.*" These were lyrics from a lovely Francis Cabrel song. "I'll hang your portrait on the ceilings of all the palaces." There are advantages to not speaking the same language.

But then the guy who sells hummus next to the butcher shop taught him a few choice English phrases, and he came home to ask, "What is dirty sex?"

"You're not going to find out."

While he learned on the fly and spoke English better every

day, I was still befuddled by most of what Parisian people said. I still listened to my French language podcasts, still meandered my way through my online courses, and still flipped through my offline books. I still wrote out the conjugations of verbs and I still wondered if it helped. So many of these verbs that were perfectly understandable on the page were completely imperfect when uttered in the real world. Especially the imperfect tense.

Back in school when I was taking French with other English students, I was a star. When we were learning only what was put on the page in front of us, my French was not just *pas mal*, it was stellar. Even my professor said, "Janice, you speak beautifully." But then he followed with, "Now if only you could understand what you were saying."

Getting my hair cut meant that I had to rehearse in front of the mirror at home. I didn't want to screw that up. Buying a summer frock started first with remembering how to ask if I could try it on. And to ask for the price of something? Oh, forget it. If it was anything over the number sixty-nine, I was screwed. As soon as something costs anything that sounds like a really long number, I flubbed up and just kept handing over twenties until they were satisfied. Often they asked for exact change. The French *adore* exact change. When I understood what they asked for, and if I had it, I handed it over. Other times, I would stick my nose in my change purse, pretend to be scrounging through my coins, and say *Non, désolé* (no, sorry), which was really me saying, "No, sorry. I haven't got a clue what you just said. Just give me my strawberries and let me get out of here, mmmk?"

I pulled out the *Non, désolé* a lot. If someone on the street was trying to hand me a paper about the latest elections, I said *Non, désolé*. If they were trying to get me to sign a petition for AIDS, Amnesty International, Greenpeace, or whatever group was standing around with clipboards wearing the same colored shirts, they got a *Non, désolé*. A lady asking for spare change? Yep. You guessed it. *Non, désolé*.

I learned to not judge people who appeared rude. They were probably just trying to learn the language.

On one gorgeous October morning, a lady handed me a song sheet because she and her friends had gathered to sing songs by the fountain. I gave her my *Non, désolé* before I even realized what she was handing me. She replied, "*Il faut*" (roughly translated, "It is necessary" or "You must!"), and she looked disheartened by my hand gesture that accompanied my *Non, désolé*.

It was a song sheet. So I could sing songs. With a group. By a fountain. IN PARIS! So I started lightening up on my *Non, désolé*-ing.

Sometimes people on the outside remarked about how lovely and easy my life was here in Paris. Try getting alterations at your French-speaking tailor, and you'll realize that living in another country before you get the hang of the language is hard (she says as she writes in the dress she altered herself because Iwilljustdoitmyself). Every little errand took longer. Everything required rehearsal.

Most of the beautiful bookstores in Paris were *tragique* to me. Each book was an ocean filled with ideas and adventures I couldn't begin to understand. There were characters I could love inside those books. I just knew it. But alas, would we ever meet?

I wasn't even funny in French. And I still couldn't flirt in French. I was simple in French.

When Christophe discovered the word "boobies," he laughed his head off and proceeded to use the word in fits of giggles for weeks after. He thought it was the funniest word ever. Boobies! Ha ha ha! Boobies!

I wondered if I sounded like a five-year-old when I spoke French.

It wasn't all bad. For instance, you've likely heard the expression *Ooh la la*, which roughly translates to Wow, Oh My, Oh Dear. But it has another meaning. I've heard it a lot while people were haggling over chandeliers and dyed feathers at the antique fair that erected itself around the corner from my apartment. Buyers were saying Ooh la la la laaaa, which translates to Are You Frigging Kidding Me With This Price? Then the potential buyer offered up another number (which I didn't catch, naturally) and the seller pulled another Ooh la la la laaaa, which translates to You Can Go Screw Yourself And The Horse You Rode In On If You Think I'm Selling That To You For That Price, You Crook.

And when Christophe watched soccer, he stood and said, "Ooh la la la laaaa!!!," which translates to What The Heck Kind Of Call Was THAT, You Arse Ref!

The best part of this language lesson was that I already knew how to say Ooh la la la laaaa, and it worked in many instances. Ooh la la la laaaa (translated, I'm Onto Something And It's Goooood).

But communicating in relationships requires a whole other level of comprehension. So how did Christophe and I communicate with each other on the big things? We spoke *Franglish*. He spoke French and inserted the English words he knew. I did the same. And we said a lot of sentences twice in French and English. We used a mix of hand signals, words, charades, drawings, and mostly, we only said what was important. We didn't mince words. We didn't rattle on. There were no snide remarks. I let a lot of stuff roll off my back, and I suspect he did as well. And if I was triggered, I had a moment of silent reflection first to see if I was triggered by a snag in my soul or something we needed to discuss together. Usually it was a snag. I let it go. Important conversations were clear, slow, and usually took place at home because we needed a quiet room to muddle through what we were trying to say. Temperatures didn't rise quickly because we were too focused on finding the right words. Though sometimes when we were frazzled, we spoke quickly in our own language while the other one stared in silence, which looked like listening even though there was no comprehension. On a day he came home from work perturbed, the most gorgeous soliloquy of words came rolling out of his mouth. He used many words that were not in my French *livre*. I stared back and nodded, all the while wondering where I could find a French dictionary of swear words. When he finished, I said, *"Bière?"* He sighed, smiled, and nodded as I handed him a bottle. I didn't need to know what he had said. I understood.

Still, it can be a drag learning a new language, especially when it's motivated by something other than the joy of learning the language. French is so *not* Italian. The Italian language is like Italian food. A feast for the tongue. Every word a spicy meatball. Every intonation a perfectly prepared noodle. Every expression a full-flavored sauce. I loved the Italian language for the sake of it. It wouldn't get me much further than directions to a great meal in Rome, but I didn't care because I love it unconditionally. I loved it because it was so easy to love. *They pronounce all the letters in a word. Bliss!*

So while my motivation for learning Italian stems from a love of the language, my motivation to learn French stemmed from loving a man. I didn't study French for the love of it. I studied it because I wanted to know what my boyfriend said to me. It was all love, but one was more indirect than the other, which made sitting down to a podcast or language CD challenging, especially when I could be outside discovering the delicacies of Paris.

But I pulled on my big girl pants and sat myself down to listen to my French language CDs and to wrap my tongue around new words. I listened to each language lesson twice. The first time through, I wanted to cry. I just didn't understand anything. The second time through, I started to get the hang of it, which encouraged me to move on to the lesson, which I listened to and went back to not understanding anything again. It was a vicious little cycle. Each day I would furrow my brow and make funny faces as I tried to pronounce the multisyllabic words.

Every time I wanted to give up, I thought of my nieces. They were learning all the time. They could learn new words, how to run the DVD player, and how to take photos with the camera apps on smartphones. And all in one day. I couldn't even cobble a sentence together with confidence. I could take a class but I still had residual trauma from office life. I couldn't seem to bring myself to sign up for anything that required that I sit in one desk for a specified amount of time.

Some days, when my brain was a tangled ball of yarn, trying to unravel the mysteries of the *passé composé* and the *conditional*, I got tense and looked over at my dusty suitcase in the corner. I could just go.

One evening, after a particularly grueling language lesson, I joined Christophe at the bar. I finished my beer while he was nursing his.

"Are you almost ready to go?" I asked.

"Not yet." He took a small sip.

This grimy bar was filled with smelly men. I was tired and on the verge of needing *la toilette* though I knew that the bathroom was wretched, as most of them are in Paris. The bar was loud that night too. I sat in silence next to Christophe, who was quite happily listening to music and taking in the scene around him. I thought back to Ben and how it would have been so easy to make a move on him that night in London. We talked so well together. In English! I could have just kissed the guy, fired off a *Dear Christophe* email, and figured out how to be the *Early Show* and live harmoniously with *Late Night*. Life could have been easier. Or even Marco or Sandro? I could have tried harder. I could have won them over. They all spoke English. Why was I with someone I couldn't even talk with in this dark, dank, loud bar? What have I done to get here, and how could I get out?

My inner escape artist pursed her lips and slanted her eyes. Game on?

No, *non. Non.*

"Okay. Ready?" Christophe was done with his beer.

We walked home. I brushed my teeth and crawled into bed to brood in silence. He sat on the stairs outside, smoking a cigarette.

"Baby! You sleep?" he yelled.

"No, not yet."

My phone rang. It was Christophe calling from the stairs. I picked up, and he started singing in his best Stevie Wonder that he just called to say he loved me. He just called to say how much he cared. He just called to say he loved me and he meant it from the bottom of his heart.

I laughed.

It was enough.

The escape artist drifted off.

He sang the song from the stairs to the bedroom and crawled into bed. I looked over at him and told him I saw Stevie Wonder at a grocery store in Los Angeles once.

"Really?" he asked.

"Yes. But he didn't see me."

It was the first time I fell asleep to the sound of him giggling.

October
2012
Paris

Dear Áine,

The weather does not know what to do with itself at this time of the year in Paris. One day its hot and humid, the next its cold and wet – and some days its both. But that doesn't keep me from exploring – as long as I dress in layers and have my umbrella handy. A scarf is also key – and très french!

Dear Áine,

The weather doesn't know what to do with itself at this time of the year in Paris. One day it's hot and humid, the next it's cold and wet—and some days it's both. But that doesn't keep me from exploring—as long as I dress in layers and have my umbrella handy. A scarf is also key, and très French!

Though the air seems confused, the earth knows exactly what to do with autumn. Squash is the super star at the market these days. I am happy to report that the vendors use the English word for butternut squash. So that's one less word I need to worry about. Learning the French language is coming along—slower than I'd prefer, but steady. Some days I feel like I've got it, and other days I feel like I'll never get it. Just as the weather volleys between summer and autumn, I volley between comprehension and confusion. But as each day gets shorter, my vocabulary list gets longer. I hope to understand all of it someday—or even most of it. In the meantime, I'm taking a break from studying and making butternut squash soup instead. The weather may not know what to do with itself in autumn, but I've got a few ideas on how to get through the season.

À bientôt!
Janice

22

Haunted by Hemingway

I was sitting outside the Louvre, eating *les macarons* from the famous patisserie Ladurée. When I first told people I was living in Paris, those that had been insisted I get a macaron. I wondered why all the fuss, but I stopped by the store to appease my Paris-loving friends. Plus, I reasoned, if the macaron was a bust, there was a plaque just down the street from Ladurée that showed the building where Oscar Wilde lived and died so I could cross it off my tourist checklist, which was getting shorter the longer I stayed in Paris.

Ages ago, a pastry chef named Pierre Desfontaines (and grandson of the founder Louis-Ernest Ladurée) came up with the brilliant notion of taking two cookies and gluing them together with a ganache filling. The result was a delicate meringue cake on the outside with a gooey jam, icing, or chocolate on the inside. The original Oreo, if you will. When eaten, the combination of their texture and flavor does a little dance in your mouth. Desfontaines also opened a tearoom for ladies. Up until then, cafés were the domain of men. Can you imagine? Now women could meet at a fancy tearoom rather than at their homes. Generations have been re-creating his culinary masterpiece ever since, and Ladurée tearooms have popped up around the city (and at Harrod's in London). I stopped by the location on corner rue Bonaparte and rue Jacob in the 6e arrondissement. The window display was a storybook theme with rainbows and topiary trees of macaron, a veritable fantasyland that lured me in as it would for Hansel and Gretel. Once inside, the busy well-coifed worker bees behind the counter buzzed around, gathering a macaron for patrons shouting flavors. *Vanille! Pistache! Chocolat!*

I bought myself a collection of six to take home for dessert with Christophe.

With the afternoon free, I walked over the bridge and through the courtyard of the Louvre. Sitting on a bench, I gazed over at I. M. Pei's glass pyramid, and I gazed down at my petite package of sweet cookies. I gazed back at the pyramid. I gazed back down at my cookies. I ripped open the package and chose the salted caramel first. The delicate meringue shell was barely able to hold itself together, which was exactly how I felt on my first bite. The sweet caramel mingled perfectly with hints of salt crystals to create a party on my palate. Dance in my mouth? Indeed.

The next was pistachio. I was starting to understand why people get more than one. They were so light and fluffy that after I ate the first, I thought I just imagined it. Before I realized it, my six macarons were gone. Christophe didn't have much of a sweet tooth anyway.

I pulled out my map, my constant companion, and with my finger, traced a route back to my neighborhood. A man approached me and asked me something in French. I looked up and uttered "ummm…ahhh," which is the universal language for "I speak English and not French." I know this because he immediately changed languages and said, "You speak English?"

Relieved to not be forced into trying to converse in or understand French, I said yes. He had asked if I needed directions. Since I was sitting outside the Louvre with my map in hand and a Ladurée bag at my side, I had the typical tourist look. His name was Frederic and wouldn't you know it, he and I were going in the same direction and he'd be happy to accompany me part of the way. Later, I wondered about this moment. I wondered if Frederic walked by the Louvre every night after work to look for a girl holding a map, then accompanied her to wherever she happened to be going.

He looked to be about my age and spoke English. He asked me if I knew anything about California as he was traveling there on vacation. Did I ever. So I looked around at the crowded street and decided to accept his invitation to walk halfway home. We took a circuitous route, which set off alarm bells, but he assured me that it was to show me the blue door at the house on rue du Cardinal-Lemoine where Hemingway lived.

Frederic had a kind look about him. Well-coifed blond hair and a little pudgy around the middle. His face looked too small for his head, but he had that look of a boy whose mother says, "I don't know why he's not married yet. He's so handsome." And whoever she is talking to sits in silence, knowing exactly why he's not married yet: his face-to-head ratio. But no one wants to say that because he takes after his mother. Still, Frederic seemed harmless, and I was trying to put out of my mind how this scene could have the makings of an *ABC Afterschool Special*. Hesitant, but intrigued by the promise of an interesting tourist site, I continued my walk with Frederic up to Hemingway's door, which was indeed blue and sported the typical sign that states he lived here. These signs were scattered throughout the city. It seems anybody who was anybody carved out time to do something brilliant in Paris.

Hemingway claimed that the best years in his life were those in Paris. He famously stated, "There are only two places in the world where we can live happy: at home and in Paris." I hoped he was right about that.

True to Frederic's promise of walking halfway home, he bid me farewell, thanked me for the information about Los Angeles, and dropped me just up the street from Hemingway's famous front door in a roundabout courtyard called Place de la Contrescarpe. Hemingway called this place "the cesspool of rue Mouffetard," but that was in the 1920s when this area was considered the dodgy side of town. Now it's one of the most coveted areas to live in Paris.

I lingered at a Café Delmas and ordered a beer. A giant beer arrived, costing 8 euro. How did one order the little beers that everyone else was drinking? I didn't realize at the time that *demi* was the magic word. Asking for a *demi* beer meant you didn't get a giant beer that sloshed about in your belly on your walk home, threatening the strength of your bladder.

I sat and tried to imagine Hemingway's point of view. In the middle of this courtyard was a fountain where a homeless man sat, murmuring loudly to himself or his imaginary friend. On the other side of the fountain, pigeons flocked in a manic uprising. Someone had tossed them a croissant, and they were tearing it to shreds. A group of teenagers in skinny jeans stood nearby puffing cigarettes and checking their phones. And a man leaned against a wall, playing "When the Saints Go Marching In" with his recorder.

In the coming days, I purchased Hemingway's *A Moveable Feast* at Shakespeare & Company, a memoir of his days in Paris during the 1920s. He was married to his first wife, Hadley, and it was here where they had their son, Bumby. The book was written with excerpts of journals found in a Louis Vuitton trunk he had left and forgotten in the basement of the Ritz Hotel in Paris years before. What a magical moment that must have been. To find his daily musings from the time in his life he loved most, like lost love letters from a bygone day. He described his daily life of trying to write importantly. He also ran in a circle of influential American expats. After World War I, the French franc plunged, making the U.S. dollar stronger. Thousands of Americans flocked to Paris, including heavy hitters of the 1920s literary scene such as Ezra Pound, F. Scott Fitzgerald, James Joyce, and Gertrude Stein.

He opened the book with, "If you are lucky enough to have lived in Paris as a young man, then wherever you go for the rest of your life, it stays with you, for Paris is a moveable feast." I thought back to my macaron picnic at the Louvre.

He had arrived in Paris after World War I, along with his new bride Hadley. He spent much of his time in Paris haunted by his desire to write important prose. He had come here as a journalist for the *Toronto Star*, but really wanted to make a go of a novelist's life. In the book, he gave many clues to live successfully as an artist in Paris, which just so happened to be what I was trying to do.

"The only thing that could spoil a day was people, and if you could keep from making engagements, each day had no limits." He spoke of the dangers of overindulging with drink while writing and of his frustrations with F. Scott Fitzgerald, who seemed to be doing just that. Perhaps Fitzgerald didn't know the word *demi*.

When it came to putting in a good day of work, Hemingway always stopped when he had a little something more to add for the next day. "I always worked until I had something done and I always stopped when I knew what was going to happen next. That way I could be sure of going on the next day." And when nothing came, he walked. There seems to be a bar or café made famous by his patronage about a thirty-minute walk from his front door in multiple directions. Why? I'm guessing that he left the house, walked for half an hour to get the creative juices flowing, sat at a café with a pencil and paper to write, then he zipped home to type it all up. "I would walk along the quais when I had finished work or when I was trying to think something out. It was easier to think if I was walking and doing something or seeing people doing something that they understood." Still, when nothing came, he had conversations with himself just as I had with Mr. Miyagi. "I would stand and look out over the roofs of Paris and think, 'Do not worry. You have always written before and you will write now. All you have to do is write one true sentence. Write the truest sentence that you know.' So finally I would write one true sentence, and then go on from there." Good to know. Thanks for the tips, Hemingway.

You're welcome.

On days that the rain would whip around buildings, I stayed home and sifted through my blog posts from the year before, trying to reshuffle, edit, add, and create something out of this raw material. When I was stuck, I called in my own imaginary Ernest Hemingway. I opened my journal and asked him for guidance. I wrote a question, then on the next line, I wrote "Hemingway:" and he answered in a voice that was my voice but also not my voice, similar to Mr. Miyagi and Percy Kelly. It was a voice that seemed wiser than myself. And that guy set me straight. He didn't mince words. He asked me why on earth I wanted to go through my blog posts from a time when I was so miserable in Los Angeles during a time when I was so happy in Paris. Good point, Hemingway. Good point. Onward.

Dear Áine,

There is this blue door I walk by often on my walks through Paris. It looks like an ordinary blue door, but this is the blue door at 74 rue du Cardinal-Lemoine, the first Paris residence of Hemingway back when he was just Ernest. Before the novels, before the accolades, before the fall, he was trying to build a new life here with is new wife Hadley and their son Bumby. And Hadley, she was building a happy family despite the cold Paris winters, post-war conditions, and tight budget. They had a nice handful of literary friends—James Joyce, F. Scott Fitzgerald, and Gertrude Stein to name a few—and the charms of Paris itself to weave into the narrative of their lives. He would go on to write books that changed literature forever, culminating in a Nobel Prize. She likely never suspected that she would go on to be known as the first wife. As I look up at the building, I imagine these newlyweds trying to make a go of it. If you walk by at twilight, you can hear doors opening and closing, friendly murmurs of conversation, and the smell of dinner on the stove. I wonder if it's Ernest and Hadley haunting the place.

"We ate well and cheaply and drank well and cheaply and slept well and warm together and loved each other." Hemingway, A Moveable Feast.

Janice

Dear Áine,

There is this blue door I walk by often on my walks through Paris. It looks like an ordinary blue door, but this is the blue door at 74 rue du Cardinal Lemoine, the first Paris residence of Hemingway back when he was just Ernest. Before the novels, before the accolades, before the fall, he was trying to build a new life here with his new wife Hadley and their son Bumby. And Hadley, she was building a happy family despite the cold Paris winters, post war conditions and tight budget. They had a nice handful of literary friends - James Joyce, F. Scott Fitzgerald and Gertrude Stein to name a few — and the charms of Paris itself to weave into the narrative of their lives. He would go on to write books that changed literature forever, culminating in a Nobel Prize.

She likely never suspected that she would go on to be known as the first wife.

As I look up at the building, I imagine these newlyweds trying to make a go of it. If you walk by at twilight, you can hear doors opening and closing, friendly murmurs of conversation, and the smell of dinner on the stove. I wonder if it's Ernest and Hadley haunting the place.

Janice

"We ate well and cheaply and drank well and cheaply and slept well and warm together and loved each other." Hemingway, A Moveable Feast

23

Guests Galore

Paris is the most popular tourist destination in the world, so if you live here, you have pretty good odds of meeting up with some vacationing cronies from your old life. If so, you'll do a lot of tour guiding, especially if you don't have the steady office job to get you out of it. *Karma is a sneaky minx.*

Generally, I was fine with walking my old friends around my new Paris, but soon I realized just how expensive it was for me to do so. Taking a day to tour them around meant not making traction on my artistic pursuits, plus paying for my own lunches and dinners in restaurants. Over time, it dawned on me that they weren't just in Paris to see me. They were looking for a free tour guide. Resentment bubbled up. *Did I really choose these friends back in my old life? Were they always this clueless?* And two thoughts kept coming up: *Why am I not saying anything?* and *How did I let this happen?* After I took one such guest to a dinner party and he proceeded to fill his wineglass with the last of the good wine without filling other glasses first, I knew I would have to create major boundaries with guests in the future. I couldn't keep this up.

Melanie explained how to regard future requests for tours around Paris. We were out for coffee the day after my old friend drank up the wine at the dinner party. She took a napkin from the table and said, "This is your life." She folded it in half. "Half of it goes to work." She folded it again. "You're left with one half that is devoted to life maintenance: groceries, paying bills, that kind of thing." She held up the small square that remained. "This small square is your free time. Do you really want to give this small square to a clueless friend from your old life who acts like a barbarian at dinner parties in your new life?"

Lesson learned.

But for the select guests who were worthy of that small square, I had developed an itinerary that would get them to all the major sites in as few steps as possible. One must be mindful of one's feet when traipsing around Paris. For this, I included a boat ride along the Seine that went from Jardin des Plantes, near my apartment, to the Eiffel Tower and back again, stopping near all the major monuments along the way. During these boat trips, something magical started to happen. As we floated along from monument to monument, my fatigued travelers would begin to open up about their frustrations about daily life: their jobs, their love lives, their grief and failures. One by one, they would talk it out, and I would listen. I didn't plan this, but each time it was the same. I think it was the lull of the boat: its slow sway and humming motor combined with the pause from dodging scooters, looking for signs, and grasping maps. Somewhere along the way, I had turned from being a Vacation Request Coach to being a Vacation Release Coach. My new vocation suited me.

But my three-day itinerary fell away with Akemi. She arrived and spent all her mornings in bed in the hotel and all her afternoons with me on my street. She had a mean case of burnout from the advertising agency. I understood all too well, so instead of walking all over the city, we just took the boat ride along the Seine. As we floated under the bridge by Notre Dame, she confessed, "I'm just so tired." And she meant it. She herself had been silently working through her own escape plans since I left.

Soon after, my mother arrived for her two-week vacation.

On the second day, she fell on a sidewalk and required two rows of stitches in her knee. We spent the night in the emergency room with Christophe as our translator. Sometimes she acted like a frail old grandma, holding my arm as we walked and telling me how this cramped and that ached. But then there were times when I saw that it was mostly an act. She was much stronger than she admitted. The day after she fell in Paris, all she needed was a few Advil and a fresh bandage each morning before she walked with me all over the city. She also slipped in questions here and there about me finding a job, but then I told her that for now, I had enough money.

"And for later?"

I shrugged and she started praying.

I'm pretty sure she mentioned her worries to my uncles and aunts who arrived one after another. I became tour guide to them all. They each mentioned that I should make a profession of touring people around the city, but when I started replying to their questions about French history with, "Dunno, Google it," they piped down about the tour guiding.

Still, they had a point. Since I spent most of my days on long hikes throughout Paris, I thought that perhaps I could get paid for it. I asked Vicki for advice. She was a painter from San Francisco. She arrived in Paris from time to time to paint scenes of rue Mouffetard. Each morning, she unfolded her artist chair on the sidewalk, pulled out her supplies, and started painting. Alongside her easel was a box of postcards of her previous paintings that she sold to those gawking over her shoulder. And since one needs a permit for such things and she *may* not have had one, she *may* have had her friend Monique come by and watch for the coppers. Monique *may* have been a Communist spy in her youth, so this side gig *may* have been a perfect fit. Vicki packed an extra guest chair for when company arrived. These two lovely silver-haired beauties chatted and sat at different locations up and down the street. Vicki painted. Monique spied. Everyone was happy. I thought Vicki was in her mid-fifties but wasn't sure because something came over her the longer she sat and painted. She seemed to regress in age as the weeks went by. I thought perhaps it was the company she kept. She stayed at a youth hostel called Young and Happy. "I'm not young, but I'm happy," she quipped when I mentioned her mysterious age regression. By the end of her Paris visits, she always had a skip in her stride of someone half her age.

On the morning before I was about to meet friends of friends and give them a little tour around the city, I stopped by Vicki who was painting a picture of the restaurant Le Verre à Pied on rue Mouffetard. She saw me coming and unfolded her guest stool. I sat and sighed, telling her I was taking some friends of friends around town for the day. "Vicki, I need to make more cash, and people have recommended becoming a tour guide. What do you think?"

"You couldn't pay me enough," she said. "But I'm a *plein air* painter. That's what I do. I like to show people Paris through my paintings." She daubed her brush in burnt amber. "With the exception of the few people such as yourself whom I allow to sit near me, I want to be left the hell alone to do what I love doing."

She was like a wise owl.

"Here's what you can do. Take my advice or leave it. Today when you tour these people around, pretend it's a paid gig. See if you're into it."

So when I met up with the friends of friends, I tried out being a tour guide. Paris was their first European city, or their first trip outside a resort or off a cruise ship. This meant they wore pretty but inappropriate footwear and yoga pants (never do this in Paris unless you're actually going to yoga or are alone in your home) and carried large, heavy water bottles. Their first request was a big coffee so they could sip and stroll. I told them that it's not easy to find a coffee to go, but then they spotted a

Starbucks on the horizon and got excited. They ordered their giant mocha-frappa-etceteras and we began exploring, me knowing that they would require *les toilettes* in twenty minutes. There are public toilets in Paris, but not that many and they are…well, public toilets, and come with all the usual unpleasantries. In order to use a toilet in a restaurant or café, one must saddle up to the bar and order something. Usually, this was an espresso, because it was cheap and really what we were after was restroom privileges. So they slurped back their espressos, headed to the loo, and in twenty minutes, they needed to do it all over again.

The French avoid this entire cycle. I figured out how they do it. They sip liquids constantly at home, likely because they are severely dehydrated in their tour around the city. They stop half an hour before their next jaunt around town. They leave the house slightly thirsty but confident they'll not need a pit stop on their tour. And when the ladies have earned restroom privileges in a café, they take them. Men? I know what they do by evidence on sidewalks.

With these friends of friends, I gave them a few facts about me, and they gave a few facts about them. It was like a first date except we all knew our relationship was fleeting and it was unlikely we'd ever meet again. I spewed off a few facts and figures about Paris as we walked around. They seemed slightly interested but would likely retain nothing except what their cameras captured. They talked about work-related ailments and stresses and especially how tired and busy they were all the time. These people were kind of a drag, but I agreed to meet them, largely out of the kindness I felt for people like Sandro and Marco when I was traveling, and because I, on this particular day, was testing to see if I would like tour guiding.

After my pleasant enough but exhausting tour around the city, I returned to Vicki who was still sitting in her artist chair on the sidewalk, putting her finishing touches on a painting. She saw me coming and whipped out her guest stool. She doesn't keep it out for fear of inviting unwanted guests. I sat.

"Well, how'd it go?" she said.

"I'm tired and over it. I didn't ask for cash but they gave me some to thank me."

"So you even got paid and still didn't like tour guiding."

I nodded.

"Sounds to me like it's not an equal exchange. How much cash would it take to make it an equal exchange?"

"Too much," I responded.

"It's settled then," she said, slapping her knee. "You're just like me. Show people Paris by selling more of those letters of yours and forget the touring." She pointed at her box of post-cards and winked. "I sell enough of these postcards to pay for my whole vacation."

And that's when Quit Your Day Job came along.

Dear Áine,

Even though there are four seasons in Paris, it seems to be the rainy season all year long. And though the tourist season is technically early summer, they seem to be here all year long too. Lately, I've become the Ambassador of Directions to confused map-gripping vacationers. But if I come upon a tour group, I usually slink my way around to quickly get where I want to be.

All the tourists eventually arrive at la pièce de résistance: the Eiffel Tower. Only here do I hover close to the groups, who are usually led by a person carrying a large plastic flower that is easily visible for anyone who meanders too far from the pack. The leader usually rattles off facts and figures about the world's most recognized monument. I don't pay much attention. Instead I listen in to people's conversations. It's easy to do and I can't resist. As we all look up into the brown belly of iron, I hear wives talking about the campaign to convince their husbands to come to Paris. I hear employees talking about the vacation time they had to earn. And students who saved every dime and are willing to eat crêpes on the street for every meal just to be here in this moment.

It takes some effort to get where you want to be. Now that they are in Paris looking at the tower they've imagined for so long, they sigh with satisfaction, snap a photo, and look for that big plastic flower to find their way home.

Au revoir!
Janice

Dear Áine,

Even though there are only four seasons in Paris, it seems to be the rainy season all year long. And though the tourist season is technically early summer, they seem to be here all year long too.

Lately, I've become the Ambassador of Directions to confused map-gripping vacationers. But if I come upon a group tour, I usually slink my way around to quickly get where I want to be.

All the tourists eventually arrive at la pièce de résistance: the Eiffel Tower. Only here do I hover close to the groups, who are usually led by a person carrying a large plastic flower that is easily visible for anyone who meanders too far from the pack. The leader usually rattles off facts and figures about the world's most recognized monument. I don't pay much attention. Instead, I listen in to people's conversations. It's easy to do and I can't resist. As we all look up into the brown belly of iron, I hear wives talking about the campaign to convince their husbands to come to Paris. I hear employees talking about the vacation time they had to earn. And students who saved every dime and are willing to eat crêpes on the street for every meal just to be here in this moment. It takes some effort to get where you want to be. Now that they are in Paris looking at the tower they've imagined for so long, they sigh with satisfaction, snap a photo and look for that big plastic flower to find their way home.   Au revoir!   Janice.

24

The Etsy Quit Your Day Job Article

A blogger from Etsy contacted me and asked if she could feature me on the Quit Your Day Job blog. This is the same blog I scoured for ideas on how I could quit the advertising agency. It featured people who successfully moved on from the daily grind to build successful businesses on Etsy. Back then, I wanted to be one of those people. Now I would be! Being featured on Etsy was the moment that changed my grassroots business that paid for my coffee and cheese addictions into a business that could also help me keep padding my buffer of cash and saving up for the next big adventure, whatever that might be.

By now, I had sent out over one thousand letters. But a week into the Quit Your Day Job article, I was getting orders to send out thousands more and I was pedaling *dans la choucroute*, which means pedaling in sauerkraut—getting nowhere fast. I went to bed at night with fifty orders to do the next day, only to wake up to fifty more. By the time I finished those, another fifty would be waiting. Of course I was astounded, delighted, and grateful for the success of this project, but there was a brief moment when I felt I had re-created history. I felt chained to my desk and overwhelmed by creating mail.

But then I changed the pattern. Instead of being forced to sit in an office with a pile of folders, I realized I was not, in fact, required to stay at my desk. There was no boss expecting me to be there, no project managers chomping at my heel, no accountant tracking my billable hours, and no supervisor deciding whether to approve a Vacation Request form.

So in the middle of addressing an envelope, I put down my pen, slipped into my ballet flats, and went for a long, slow stroll down rue Monge. I crisscrossed my way toward the Seine, changing sides of the street wherever there was a flower shop to admire. I literally stopped to smell the roses. I slipped quietly into Saint-Nicolas-du-Chardonnet church to admire the soft glow of the chandeliers and sit among the ladies who still wore veils to cover their heads. Together we prayed in serene silence.

Amply amped up on spiritual mojo, I left the church and continued down rue des Bernardins to cross the bridge at Quai de l'Archevêché and take a gander at the locks shining in the sun. Lovers from around the world add their locks to the bridge to solidify their love. I read a few of their names and sent them a silent blessing. I hoped Karen and Rob were doing well, and Patricia and Allan too. I continued to my favorite bridge, Pont Saint-Louis, where from one spot I could see the sexy buttresses of the back end of Notre Dame, the statue-encrusted Hôtel de Ville, the boats puttering beneath the bridge, and most importantly, the violin player.

By the look of the gathering crowd, he had a gaggle of gawking groupies waiting for him to finish his set so they could have a little tête-à-tête with hopes for a little one-on-one. I could see why. His hair was tied back in a ponytail with a few wisps swaying in the breeze. He looked more like a skateboarder than a violinist, which was part of the appeal. When I dropped a few coins in his violin case, he locked eyes with me and shot me a sly grin.

He was good.

So was his music. He was an artist at play. I had spied him here before, playing to no one, swaying to the sound of his own music. When he sped up the tempo, he hopped and jived to his

own beat, making his own fun. And I guess that's what happened to me with the Paris Letters. Though I enjoyed sharing
the letters with people, I created them for myself first. I wanted
to see how the letters would turn out as much, or maybe more,
than the people who would receive them. I always had an idea
of how to start and of what to say, but as I spent more time with
each letter, I was really just being witness to what happened
when the colors mixed. And I was never sure what words would
come out of me until I picked up the pen and started to write.

We—the violin player and me—were not so dissimilar.
Artists amusing themselves first for the sake of it.

Artists.

It had only occurred to me in that moment that I was indeed
an artist. In Paris! The wish I had in January 2010 had come
true. It was a circuitous route, so circuitous in fact that I didn't
even catch what was going on until this moment on the bridge.
I had to first become an escape artist, then travel to discover the
work of Percy Kelly and settle into a life that was conducive to
creating art. And along the way, I found the lovely Christophe.

I was an artist!

When my beautiful violinist had finished, the salivating sisters
chatted with him as he packed away his violin. Bidding them
adieu with a tip of his hat, he headed toward the accordion
player who had started playing on the other end of the bridge.
He stopped and listened for a minute. He tossed a few coins in
the hat and disappeared in the crowd.

I skipped toward home. I had orders to fill.

Dear Áine,

Notre Dame turns 850 this year. She's looking fantastique for her age. How French of her. Paris has grown out from this Gothic masterpiece of gurgling gargoyles and flying buttresses. And the English King, Henri VI, was crowned king of France here (Mon Dieu!), and later Napoleon was crowned Emperor here. Now, Notre Dame peers out to the green waters of the Seine, standing tall for the constant stream of tourists snapping photos from the riverboats. To celebrate her birthday, she's getting a new set of bells. The originals were melted down to make cannonballs during the French Revolution. The replacements were temporary and always out of tune. I had the chance to see the new bells up close before they were hoisted to the towers. First, they were paraded through Paris on flatbed trucks, then displayed inside on the cathedral floor. Each bell is named after a different saint and tuned to the only original bell called Emmanuel, which was the bell Quasimodo liked best and would swing from with delight. Despite all this bell hoopla, they are silent in the days leading up to Easter. Apparently, all the church bells of France grow wings and fly to Rome to get a special Easter blessing from the Pope. On Easter Sunday, they return and drop chocolates all over France. So while children in other countries have their eyes on the ground, hoping to catch a glimpse of the Easter Bunny, French children look to the skies for falling chocolate. I, however, head straight to les chocolateries.

Janice

Dear Áine,

Notre Dame turns 850 this year. She's looking fantastique for her age. How French of her. Paris has grown out from this Gothic masterpiece of gurgling gargoyles and flying buttresses. And the English King, Henry VI, was crowned King of France here (Mon Dieu!), and later Napoleon was crowned Emperor here. Now, Notre Dame peers out to the green waters of the Seine, standing tall for the constant stream of tourists snapping photos from the riverboats. To celebrate her birthday, she's getting a new set of bells. The originals were melted down to make cannonballs during the French Revolution. The replacements were temporary and always out of tune. I had the chance to see the new bells up close before they were hoisted to the towers. First, they were paraded through Paris on flatbed trucks, then displayed inside on the cathedral floor. Each bell is named after a different saint and tuned to the only original bell, called Emmanuel, which was the bell Quasimodo liked best and would swing from with delight. Despite all this bell hoopla, they are silent in the days leading up to Easter. Apparently, all the church bells of France grow wings and fly to Rome to get a special Easter blessing from the Pope. On Easter Sunday, they return and drop chocolates all over France. So while children in other countries have their eyes on the ground, hoping to catch a glimpse of the Easter Bunny, French children look to the skies for falling chocolate. I, however, head straight to les chocolateries.

   Janice

25

Yellow Flip-Flop Summer

The following summer in Paris felt like the longest I'd had since my yellow flip-flop summer, which was the summer I was too young to work on my uncle's farm but old enough to stay home and look after my younger sister Carla. I wore yellow flip-flops nearly every day and had tan marks on the top of my feet well into the next February to prove it. Free time was as plentiful as the humidity and mosquitoes. We had full days to ourselves except for an hour in the late morning when Grandma came over to tend the garden we shared in our backyard.

Grandma wasn't one for a lot of chitchat when I was a kid. English was her second language. She and my grandfather had immigrated to Canada from Belgium after the war with their three children. Once they settled in, they had three more children, including my mom. I thought about my grandma a lot during those long, easy summer days of writing letters in Paris. Letter-writing was the only way for her to communicate with her family. There were no phones for her first years in Canada. She lived for word from her sisters and mother. In fact, she arranged with the postmaster that if a letter from Belgium had arrived, he would honk twice at the mailbox upon delivery. She would run out right away. If there was no honk, it was just bills and she could collect them later.

If I had a typical photo of my grandma, it would be of her in the garden. She'd be wearing a long sundress, bent over with her rear end high in the air, pulling out weeds between the onions. That was my grandma.

She never fully grasped English but she was clear. She had commands for after eating lunch: "Go wash your hands. Don't touch the walls." And commands for in the car: "No feets on the seats." And my favorite command: "Have it to me," when she would want me to give her something. She never quite mastered when to use the verbs "to have" and "to give." I never corrected her because it made it easier to imitate her later.

Though we didn't rattle on together, Grandma and I had a common language in the garden. My childhood homestead was largely self-sustaining, a side effect from those who grew up during the war. We would heat our home with wood my dad cut himself. We made our own maple syrup, canned fruit from our orchard, and made a wide variety of culinary concoctions out of what we grew in our garden.

Most summer mornings, Grandma would barrel up the driveway to toil in the garden. I'd be sitting on the step petting kittens and ask her, "Flip-flops or running shoes?" Flip-flops were fine to wear in the garden for most jobs except for hoeing weeds, which required running shoes.

She'd nod hello and say, "Flip-flops. Grab a basket. Beans today." And we'd head out to the garden to pick beans. Sometimes the row of green beans was eternal. You'd be surprised just how many beans you can get from one plant.

I'd whine, "Grandma, why did we plant so many beans?"

She'd reply, "You'll be happy you did in November. Happier still in February. Keep picking."

When I picked carrots, I'd ask, "Grandma, why are some carrots short and some long? Especially when we planted them all at the same time?"

She'd reply, "Some days are short and some long but they are all the same time. That's just how it is."

Sometimes zucchini would grow huge, literally overnight. "Wow, Grandma. Look at this." I'd hold up a two-foot-long zucchini. "It's ginormous!"

She'd reply, "Don't get too excited. Bigger zucchinis aren't as good as the smaller ones." I didn't understand this until much later in life.

Grandma would explain that some crops were ready to harvest early for a reason, like radishes, which were always ready first even if you pretty much ignored them. "Radishes come up first so you have strength for the growing season. As the season goes by, you get stronger and stronger so you can carry the heavy pumpkins, which are the last to harvest."

"Grandma! You're just joking."

"See if I'm right. See if the radishes come up first and the pumpkins come up last. Then you tell me why that is. God doesn't make mistakes."

Once we had weeded what needed weeding and picked what needed picking, we went to the kitchen to prepare it for winter. I would cut this and that and have it to her. She would blanch this and that. I'd carry the jars of tasty vittles down to the cellar. And she was right about those beans. I was always glad to have them in November and especially glad in February.

One year, right before I left for university, Grandma departed this life. But not until after pumpkin harvest.

I can't even believe this life I had. It seemed like so much work back then. But now, it all seems charming. Now when I dream of my future, it includes a garden. Perhaps someday, I will be the one in a sundress, bent over with my rear end in the air, pulling out the weeds between the onions.

"Grandma, why is this row of beans so crooked?"

"So I can fit more plants in it. Keep picking."

By the end of summer in Paris, the markets were flooded with fruits and vegetables. Each Sunday, I walked to the market at Place Monge with Melanie, who by now had become one of my closest friends in Paris. We hardly spoke, knowing what was coming: natas for breakfast. Upon arrival at the market, we beelined for our favorite stall and ordered two of these famous vanilla-custard-filled tartlets from Portugal to eat *en place*. With our eyes closed, standing one step out of line, we were transported far away to a culinary paradise where clouds were made of puff pastry.

When we opened our eyes, we scanned the market. We always started at the vegetable guy who smiled wide on approach, I suspect because when I first met him, I started talking with him in the informal *Tu* form rather than the more appropriate *Vous* form reserved for supervisors, strangers, and vegetable salesmen. He smiled and winked. Since I talked with Christophe in the *Tu* form, I was constantly making politeness mistakes with others. But in this case, the mistake was in my favor as the vegetable guy usually handed me a few berries to taste while I picked out *les légumes* for the week.

When I first met Melanie, I didn't realize the prize I was getting. Upon further observation, I saw that she was a shiny bauble. She had big curls that bounced as she walked, catching the glance of salivating men everywhere. Her skin had a creamy glow, as if it was lit from within like a delicate parchment lampshade. She was exactly my height, so when we kissed *bonjour* on each cheek, we had, at times, slammed cheekbones.

The olive guy nearly fell over when we arrived at his booth. He clutched his chest in mock heartache. He then scooped Melanie's black olives before she could even ask for them, preferring instead to use their precious little time together to ask her out yet again. She laughed and politely declined *encore*. He clutched his chest *encore*. On occasion, when I went to the market without her, he berated me with questions about where she might be spending her time when so very clearly she should be at the market buying olives and allowing him the pleasure of beholding her glowing visage.

Over at another cheese booth was a young red-headed student who practiced his English with me while I practiced my French with him. I tried to ask questions in French. He politely corrected me and answered me in English, after which I politely corrected him. For months, I enamored my taste buds with chèvre, the tangy rounds of goat cheese. They ranged from stinky to very stinky. As my French improved, I could ask him more questions about more cheeses. Eventually, we started talking about the harder cheeses and especially the delicious cream-colored bricks of *comté*. One day I hope to make it further in my language skills to ask about the mysteries of the Roqueforts, marbled with various shades of blue.

Our last stop at the market was the flower guy, who wrapped our baton bouquets in waxy brown paper. We hauled our load back to *la rue* where we stopped at the Tourn'Bride café for a coffee. Sitting at the side of the bar so we could store our treasures along the wall, I ordered a *crème*, "*Mais pas beaucoup de crème*," marveling when it arrived in my preferred shade of camel.

Next stop was the *boulangerie*, where we stood in a line thirty people long. Everyone seemed content to wait and watch, and I understood why. The bustling market street came alive on Sundays. A horn band played on the corner. Children danced as parents looked on, leaning on carts and soaking up sunshine. The beggars slouched more dramatically in an attempt to relieve people of their small change, couples walked arm in arm, with one of them holding a basket of vegetables. A basket! A tour group partook in a tasting at the *fromagerie*, and I cocked my ear to eavesdrop. At another café sat two well-coifed men in designer jeans and shiny shoes, accessorized with a matching set of droopy-lipped bulldogs who lapped up crumbs under the table. Church bells rang. Pigeons scattered.

Once at the front of the line, I ordered my baguette and an *escargot*, a donut shaped like a snail and speckled with raisins. I delivered it to Christophe who had a line of his own at his rotisserie. I thanked him for the flowers, but I said it loudly for the old ladies to hear, "*Merci pour les fleurs, mon amour!*" He always left me money on the market mornings to go pick out flowers for myself. He always leaned down from his perch and kissed me. The old ladies always swooned, clutching their hearts. "*Avec plaisir*, my darling," he would say. He winked and turned to the next customer in line.

Balancing the baguettes and bouquets, I bid Melanie *adieu* with a careful kiss on each cheek and headed home. I walked toward my door and heard the singing troupe collecting near the fountain to begin their *repertoire*. I dialed the code to my building and walked through the courtyard where I noticed the ferns had fully unfurled in the garden.

I carefully climbed the round staircase to my apartment. It was narrow and I had long-stemmed flowers. I opened my door, stepped into my kitchen, and sighed. This apartment never got bigger, but for now I could open the windows to the breeze. Sometimes I yearned for a house in the country with a yard and bedrooms big enough to have bedside tables, a bathroom with a tub, and a view of a lake. I looked out at my ferns, my geraniums, and the brick wall. For now, this was doable.

I unloaded my groceries and began dicing vegetables for soup. I had become an accomplished cook here in Paris, thanks partly due to creating days where I made time for it, partly by my desire to participate in market life rather than stand at the periphery as so many hotel-bound tourists do, and partly because I loved my cast-iron-Dutch-oven-pot-thing.

The day I walked this heavy-as-heck pot home, I realized my one-suitcase nomadic days were officially over. There is that moment in a girl's life when she makes the Dutch oven purchase. Another era hath begun. And this era hath a domestic tone. Surprisingly, I didn't mind. I actually loved this domestic aspect of myself that was emerging. As I diced vegetables, I would think back to my advertising career. I paid a lot of money to have someone else cut my vegetables. Here in Paris, it was a surprising pleasure to do it myself. And, of course, in Paris, I had the time. Sweet, rich, wonderful time to cut my own vegetables.

Bit by bit, I learned the language of the kitchen, and it occurred to me that this was how to learn a foreign language too. I proceeded to be gentle with learning to speak and to treat my new words like delicious morsels rather than trying to get something accomplished quickly and not really enjoying the process. I wish I would have known this in my old corporate job. I wish I could have known to sit in my office, look at the piles of folders, and take my time with each one rather than rush through them all. Why did I feel the need to go at the pile of folders like I was on a game show and the clock was running? The faster I would go, the more folders they would give me. And I'd get paid the same anyway. Why all the frantic days? Why the boasting about being either busy or tired but never about being happy? Oh, that old, busy, overwhelmed version of myself. I wish I could go back and tell her to calm down, slow down, and find joy in the moment. Was it me being clueless or was I steeped in an environment addicted to busy and tired? In Paris, I was in an environment that worshipped slow and delicious. And quickly, slow was becoming my preferred mode.

One day in the kitchen of my Paris flat, as my vegetable soup was simmering and I was washing a coffee cup, those summer days with my grandma came rushing back. I felt as if no time had passed. The years of corporate life in between were folded and compacted instantly into a few concise chapters rather than the long years of stress they actually were. And that's how I decided they would live in my mind for now on.

After the dishes were done and the soup was finished, I donned my flats and walked to the park across the street next to the church to sit in the sun. I noticed that the tops of my feet were getting quite *bronzé*.

Dear Áine,   March 2012, Paris

I spent the day meandering through one of Paris' flea markets. When you're an old country like France, a lot of stuff piles up. Things are passed down through the generations or are found after years of hibernation in dresser drawers or long forgotten boxes in attics. So I was not surprised to come across a pile of postcards from the turn of the century. After purchasing a stack, I zipped off to Angelina's café to take a closer look at my new acquisition

Angelina's serves the world's finest hot chocolate. It's so thick that I dare not ask of the ingredients. Stops the heart just imagining the amount of cream, sugar and chocolate it takes to make something this heavenly. The powdered concoctions of my youth should hang their heads in shame. This hot chocolate trumps them all!

ANGELINA
PARIS

Upon a closer inspection of my postcards, I noticed many from a M. Deluchar to a Mme. Martinazo. They were innocent in their messages - happy birthdays and happy new years. But the volume of postcards made me wonder if M. Deluchar had a big ol' crush on Mme. Martinazo. Was every best wish really a restrained unrequited love note? Did he agonize over his choice of postcard, hoping it conveyed a secret message of a love that could never be? For the sake of my romantic heart, I hope so. My imagination spilled over with delicious possibilities. Looking back, I wonder if I was simply drunk in love with my hot chocolate. ♡ Janice

Dear Áine,

I spent the day meandering through one of Paris's flea markets. When you're an old country like France, a lot of stuff piles up. Things are passed down through the generations or are found after years of hibernation in dresser drawers and boxes in the attic. So I was not surprised to come across a pile of postcards from the turn of the century. After purchasing a stack, I zipped off to Angelina's café to take a closer look at my new acquisition.

Angelina's serves the world's finest hot chocolate. It's so thick that I dare not ask the ingredients. My heart skips a beat just imagining the amount of cream, sugar, and chocolate it takes to make something this heavenly. The powdered concoctions of my youth should hang their heads in shame. This hot chocolate trumps them all!

Upon closer inspection of my postcards, I noticed many from a Monsieur Deluchar to a Mademoiselle Martinazo. They were innocent in their messages—happy birthdays and happy new years—but the volume of postcards made me wonder if Monsieur Deluchar had a big ol' crush on our mademoiselle. Was every best wish really a restrained unrequited love note? Did he agonize over his choice of postcards? Hope they conveyed a secret message of love that could never be? For the sake of my romantic heart, I hope so. My imagination spilled over with delicious possibilities. Looking back, I wonder if I was simply drunk in love with my hot chocolate.

Adoringly,
Janice

26

Nightmares...Les Cauchemars

Christophe shook me awake.
"*Quoi?*" I asked. What?
"*Cauchemar?*"
"*Quoi?*" I asked again.
"You know…dream…bad."
Yes. Dream. Bad. The recurring nightmare. There were slight variations but the meaning was the same. I was back in California and being offered another advertising job, but this time at quadruple the pay and with all my favorite coworkers. I thought to myself that taking this job would be a smart financial move. Suze Orman would approve. She would remind me that instead of making money during my big money-making years and contributing to my IRA, I was in Paris spending 4 euro on chai tea lattes. When converted into U.S. dollars, I was rockin' a $6 latte. Suze would not approve of this.

In the dream, Suze told me to take the job. I was considering it. Not because I wanted it, but because it would be a smart move financially. That Suze had me frazzled. If I took the job, I'd have to haul myself and my Polish Frenchman back to California and hope it would be all like *The Alchemist* or *Wizard of Oz* happy-ending-journey-worth-it.

In the dream, I walked through the halls of the advertising agency and saw my favorite studio people (Gregg! Marcus!), my favorite IT guys (Oscar! Nilesh!), account people (Joanna! Becca! Mason!), and co-conspirators—the Creatives (Akemi! Jan!). The list went on. Every person I've ever adored during office life was there waiting for me.

I sat in on a meeting. My gut started to do that weird thing it always did in meetings. The baseline stress building back up again along the back walls of my stomach. I started to sweat and wondered about the decisions I made that led me back here. How did this happen?

As everyone else talked about campaigns, I started to think about IKEA. If I moved back here, I'd have to get a lot of stuff at IKEA because I'd start with zero household items. I was not going to schlep my ladle from Paris. My cast-iron Dutch oven treasure would have to stay in Paris too. It was too heavy.

They kept talking about budgets and timing of the campaign. I started wondering how I would fit the IKEA load into the car. Oh gawd! I sold my car! I would have to buy another car and get wrangled back into that hot mess of car payments, insurance, gas, car washes, and the bait-and-switch negotiations at EZ Lube.

The meeting ended and a group lunch was suggested. Group lunches always filled me with anxiety. Someone always ordered more. Someone always ordered less. The bill was always split evenly. And resentment hung in the air as we would drive back to the office clown-car style.

It occurred to me that I always had lunch with Christophe in Paris. Didn't I? Or was that a dream? Did Paris happen? I thought I lived in Paris but now I'm not sure. Maybe I just dreamed up a life in France like Demi Moore in *Passion of Mind*.

And that's when I woke up in Paris next to Christophe, relieved that I didn't have to decide on any job, relocation, IKEA, EZ Lube, or group lunch. I was here in Paris. I could breathe again, and I did. I yawned into a full-body stretch, hopped out of bed, and skipped off to the kitchen to make him coffee for a change. And I applauded myself.

These dreams came with more frequency as time wore on, and I knew why. I'd have to leave Paris and go back to Toronto to get a more substantial visa if I was planning to live in France.

On the day I said good-bye to Christophe, he told me not to walk by the butcher shop on my way to the airport. He couldn't handle it.

Back in Toronto, I went straight to the French embassy to begin the paperwork for my new French visa. I then hopscotched between my mom's house and sister's house in the weeks I waited for the visa to be approved. Each day, Christophe called. Each day, he told me he loved me and was waiting for me to return. Each day, he would ask if the visa had arrived.

I nearly mowed down the deliveryman as he came up the driveway with my visa. Soon I was back on a plane heading for Paris. When I arrived, Christophe was at work. I walked up to him with my suitcase bumping along the cobblestones behind me. He stepped off his platform, leaned down, and gave me the biggest, best movie kiss of my life. Right there on the street! The people at the café across the street cheered. And me? I nearly cried. I never wanted to leave his side again.

So I could float for a while. No more paperwork. I could just explore, paint letters, and make sweet love to my blue-eyed dreamboat.

Back when the lady at the embassy accepted my visa application, she gave me a form with some signatures and stamps. "Send this in as soon as you get to France," she said. And she said it in English because it was important. So upon my arrival in Paris, I sent in the form and figured life moved on. Oh no. No, no. *Non.*

I soon received papers in the mail stating that I was to show up for my next visa appointment. *What the?* But this time, I was to pay 340 euro online beforehand and print out the receipt. Now, it is unpleasant when I know a bill is coming, but it is really unpleasant when it sneaks up like that. In addition to the proof-of-payment receipt, I was to show up at the visa appointment with a slew of other paperwork. So my time of relaxing and painting became a time of gathering and translating.

On the appointment day, I was herded with the rest of the crowd, who I soon learned had the same appointment time as myself, into a large room with many doors. There was an American girl in front of me, a New Zealand girl behind me, and a bilingual guy from Montreal behind her. Together, we formed our French Visa Office Alliance.

In the first room, a lady looked at our paperwork one by one and told each of us that the 340-euro fee we had paid online had increased 9 euros, so we must now go to the Tabac shop around the corner and purchase a 9-euro stamp. If this sounds confusing and inefficient, you're following. It WAS confusing and inefficient.

Lucky for me and my new alliance, I had spotted the Tabac shop on my way into the building, so despite not understanding her instructions (what word is left and what is right?), I still knew where to go. Off we went. Ten minutes later, we returned to the lady who ushered us into yellow chairs along with the rest of the parade of stamp holders.

One by one, we were called into the room of blue chairs where we sat and waited. One person at a time was called into Blue Door #1 and came out of Blue Door #2 a few minutes later and was ushered into Blue Door #3. This person soon came out of Blue Door #3 to wait until a nurse came out of Blue Door #4 with an envelope and handed it to the doctor who invited the person through Blue Door #5. From there, each person was taken back to the blue chairs to wait until being called back to the original yellow chairs to wait until called through White Door #1.

Confused? Exactly. Imagine this game in another language.

No one knew what was going on behind any of those doors because no one had been told—and if they were told, they were told in French, and 95 percent of us didn't speak French because we had all just arrived in Paris. Luckily I had the bilingual Montreal dude in my alliance and asked him questions whenever he was released from a door. Then I conveyed his information to one of the girls who came out of another door, who passed it onto the next girl if I was behind one of the blue doors. The whole room had ears perked on our little alliance of English-speaking smarty-pantses.

This sounds like grade-five antics, but we were all afraid of screwing up our visas just because we didn't know enough French. And when it comes to visas, everyone gets a little tense.

This is what happened during my musical chairs exercise...

Yellow chair: This is where you sat when they saw that you paid your 349 euros. You had already won once you were seated here, but they didn't tell you that. They called you one by one into the next room of blue chairs, which was surrounded by blue doors.

Blue Door #1: Behind this door was a nurse who looked at your chart, measured your height, and weighed you. Thank God I didn't know how to judge myself in kilos.

Blue Door #2 was the back door from Blue Door #1 to...

Blue Door #3, which was a little closet where you were told to take off all your jewelry and clothes from the waist up. My conversation with the nurse went like this after she told me to get nudie:

Me: *Tout?* All?
Nurse: *Oui. Tout.*
Me: *Zero ici.* (Me swirling my hands over my boob area)
Nurse: *Zero ici.* (Her swirling her hands over my boob area)
Me: Nothing. (In English)
Nurse: Nothing. (In English)
Me: *Vraiment?* Really?
Nurse: *Vraiment.* Really.

Me: *Oui?*
Nurse: *Oui.*

So I got nudie in the closet. On the other side of the closet was another door that another nurse opened whether I was ready or not.

Surprise Blue Door #3B was where I was pulled aggressively to the x-ray machine so they could take an x-ray of my chest. This was also where they took away the cardigan I was holding in front of my ta-tas. Chin up, arms out, stop giggling nervously, take a breath, snap, grab cardigan, go back to Blue Door #3 to re-cover your ta-tas, then go back out to the…

Blue chair outside to re-cover the rest of you. And to whisper what just happened to the chick from New Zealand.

Blue Door #4 opened with a nurse carrying your fresh x-ray to the doctor who brought you through…

Blue Door #5 for an interview. My doctor first asked "*Fumez?*" And I said, "Yes, I'm female." And pointed to the obvious outline of my boobs on my x-ray. He laughed and suggested we talk in English because this was important. He started again. Smoker? Ahhh. No. Whew. He looked at my x-ray and told me my chest looked great. *If I had a dime…* He also said I had no scarring from that bout of pneumonia from when I was a kid, which now released me from the phantom death grip I've carried for thirty years. He listened to my chest and said I sounded stressed. "Yes, this revolving door visa experience is stressful." He prescribed leaving as soon as I had my new visa stamp. Later, I prescribed myself a glass of wine to flush the stress out of my system. After the interview with the doctor, I was handed a prescription for a booster shot and was sent back to the…

Blue chair to wait for permission to sit in the original…

Yellow chair to wait more for the call through the…

White door, where a lady took my pile of paperwork that

was more or less pretty much sort of good enough but only because it was Friday and she was in a good mood. And from there, she slapped a new fancy sticker in my passport and told me I could now go through the next door...

Exit.

I was in Paris to stay. So I immediately left on vacation with Christophe to backpack through Prague, Vienna, and Budapest.

Dear Áine,

I saw a woman in a café today.
She was writing a letter. I thought to myself, Gosh its
been AGES since I wrote a letter. It hasn't actually been
so long, but it sure feels like it. I've been out of town on
vacation with Christophe. In the month of August, Paris is
a ghost town. Shops close and everyone ships out to a distant
land that promises expansive beaches and cold drinks – two
things you can't find in Paris. When you've grown accustomed to
getting tasty morsels from your local boulangerie and it closes
for a month, you become motivated to skip town too. But
now its September and I've returned to the land of pain
au chocolat. Oh joy!

Dear Áine

I saw a woman in a café today. She was writing a letter. I thought to myself, Gosh it's been AGES since I wrote a letter. It hasn't actually been so long, but it sure feels like it. I've been out of town on vacation with Christophe. In the month of August, Paris is a ghost town. Shops close and everyone ships out to a distant land that promises expansive beaches and cold drinks—two things you can't find in Paris. When you've grown accustomed to getting tasty morsels from your local boulangerie and it closes for a month, you become motivated to skip town too. But now it's September and I've returned to the land of pain au chocolat. *Oh joy!*

September is "la rentrée," which is the French version of back-to-school, except in France everyone is back from vacation. As I turn left out my front door and head up to the Seine, I see a lot of tanned shop owners sweeping out and dusting off—getting ready to reopen after a month-long sojourn. They look at peace, genuinely pleased to have basked in the sun, but also to be back doing what they do. I, too, am pleased to be back doing what I do—painting, writing, and walking.

As I walk along the Seine, I see more grinning shopkeepers turning their Fermé signs to Ouvert. I wonder if I would have stayed in my advertising career if I had the full month of August to rejuvenate and explore distant lands. Burnout was a big factor in my decision to leave. Le sigh.

Best not to think back. Take the lessons and leave the rest. And stop by la boulangerie *for a croissant. It has been far too long.*

Janice

~ 27 ~

Paris Revealed Itself to Me in Layers

When I first arrived in Paris, I took in the usual tourist sites up and down the Seine. I marveled at the Eiffel Tower. I strolled from boutique to boutique, picking up culinary treasures along the way. I sat in a lot of cafés to take in the scene. All those aspects of Paris that make it a great place to visit. Over time, Paris revealed another layer of itself: the rudeness, the homelessness, the pickpockets. Aspects of Paris that made it a terrible place to visit. And still later, more was revealed: small, quiet garden court-yards tucked just beyond the hustle of the street, tiny patisseries that only make one perfect dessert, the kindness of storekeepers when I became a regular customer. Aspects of Paris that made it a wonderful place to live.

The same was true with Christophe. As we began to learn each other's languages, we repeated our stories but with more detail. In some cases, we would ask a question about the past, and if the other didn't want to talk about it, the question would be dismissed with a wave and a *"Ma vie avant."* My life before. It wasn't important. But there were a few stories we had to tell. For example, I wanted to find out about his scars during his "Fall. Bad." And with a few more retellings (and more French lessons on my part), this aspect of his *vie avant* was revealed.

He was born in Białystok in northeastern Poland. He was the third of three boys. His dad died of cancer when he was nine years old. His mother died of kidney failure by the time Christophe was twenty. With both his brothers having families of their own, he felt he no longer had a home so he joined the army. After two years, a friend invited him to work on a construction crew in Paris. At the time, many teams of Polish men came to Paris to do renovations on old, crumbling buildings. Because of the currency exchange, they were able to make more money getting paid in Euros than at home. They came, worked, sent money home to their families, and eventually returned home themselves. Christophe took his friend up on the offer but never returned to Poland. He arrived and began working on a large renovation project. One day, while working with a team on a roof, one guy moved one way, another moved the other way, and Christophe fell three stories. He landed on his feet and one wrist, crushing them all.

He spent six months in a hospital, going through operations, recovery, and rehabilitation. His doctor said he would never walk again and if he did, he would walk with a limp and a cane.

During this time, he barely understood any French. He sat in silence as doctors and nurses discussed treatment with each other and tried to explain what was happening to him. All the other patients were French. Near the end of his stay, the doctor decided that he was young enough to go back to school while he continued with physical therapy. For three years, Christophe went to school, got an education, learned French, and rebuilt his legs and wrist.

He had a full recovery. Not only did he walk again, but he was able to do so without a limp or cane. His scars that I would eventually trace with my fingers were the only signs that he had fallen.

After school, he went back to doing renovations, finding work here and there, usually with teams from Poland. In between jobs, he befriended a butcher who was working on rue Mouffetard. The butcher had asked if he could help out at the shop for a day. Someone had quit the day before and they were down a man. Christophe agreed. The next day, he helped out at the shop, mostly roasting the chickens. That evening, the butcher offered to give him a lift home on his motorcycle and en route, they were in an accident. Christophe fell off the back and was unscathed, but the butcher broke his shoulder. Now they were down two workers at the shop, so Christophe was asked to stay on. Three years later, I waltzed down the street, sat at a café, and wrote him a letter.

Eventually, I gave him the letter and he was able to answer my questions: yes, his feet get tired, and yes, people have said he looks like Daniel Craig. He doesn't follow one soccer team in particular, but he's quite fond of teams and players from Poland. And he would be delighted to take a lifetime to piece together a conversation with me, as I am his sunshine, his only sunshine. I make him happy when skies are gray.

After our two-week romance in Paris, he wasn't sure I would return. And honestly, he wasn't sure he cared. It was a nice two weeks with a nice girl. Something to ponder and smile about later. But as the days wore on, he thought about how, since his mom died, he had been on his own. He always landed on his own two feet (sometimes painfully), but he never had to be responsible for someone beyond himself. Perhaps it would be nice to look after someone else. To dare to love and be loved. And here was this nice Canadian girl who appeared without a plan, without ties elsewhere, and though she couldn't speak much French, he didn't mind. He knew what it was like to not speak the language. And she was coming back through Paris. Perhaps he could convince her to stay "to see."

And of course, I did.

Dear Áine,

I have found the most romantic spot in Paris. It's not the Eiffel Tower, nor is it the lock bridge behind Notre Dame cathedral. It's a rose garden tucked in behind the natural history museum in Jardin des Plantes. The June sun has burned through grey skies, whispering to the flowers that it's time. Bulbous blooms burst open in every shade from crimson and violet to blush pink and white. The bees are pleased. In the breeze, a rainbow of petals floats by, caressing cheeks before stowing away in picnic bags. Statues sit or stand along the path under the rose trellises, politely posing for artists who come along to capture the scene. As I sit and paint, I wonder if the statues are aware of each other, contemplating who will make the first move.

Le sigh,

Janice

Dearest Áine,

I have found the most romantic spot in Paris. It's not the Eiffel Tower, nor is it the lock bridge behind Notre Dame Cathedral. It's a rose garden, tucked in behind the natural history museum in Jardin des Plantes. The June sun has burned through gray skies, whispering to the flowers that it's time. Bulbous blooms burst open in every shade from crimson and violet to blush pink and white. The bees are pleased. In the breeze, a rainbow of petals floats by, caressing cheeks before stowing away in picnic bags. Statues sit or stand along the path under the rose trellises, politely posing for artists who come along to capture the scene. As I sit and paint, I wonder if the statues are aware of each other, contemplating who will make the first move.

> *Le Sigh,*
> *Janice*

～ 28 ～

Beautiful Old Ladies

The surprising side effect to having a letter-writing business is that sometimes I got letters in return. Most of the time, it was old ladies. They would write, telling me that they share my letters with their knitting groups at their local library or they take them down to the cafeteria at their old-age homes and pass them around. In one instance, I received a letter from a granddaughter, informing me that the Paris Letter had arrived for her grandmother on the day she died. Though she didn't get a chance to read it, her family who surrounded her took turns silently reading the final piece of mail she would receive in this life.

After my grandfather passed away, my grandmother (on my dad's side) moved into a retirement village. She had much to say about the changes in her life. In her missives to me, Dispatches from The Home as she called them, it started to dawn on me that some people just need someone to whom they can write a letter, and I was a willing recipient.

Dear Janice,

Sorry it took longer to reply to your most interesting and colorful letter. Maybe you haven't realized this yet, but you are entertaining a large group, and of course I take some of the glory. After all, this is my granddaughter's work of art. Passed around your magazine article too. The picture of the trilliums was so real and vivid in my memories, I could nearly smell them.

I am still enjoying my laziness and getting more so, although I must have almost reached the peak. I hate to admit this, but I think I am due for the prize for the laziest person of all here. It's not a bad life at all. There are no meals to cook, no washing to do, no groceries to buy, no house to scrub. I do have to clean up around a bit. Just unable to put up with the place otherwise.

The people here are all old and as friendly as can be. There are many planned activities and lots of phys-ed. The kids subscribed me to the newspaper so I keep in touch with the world and local affairs, and of course "For Better or Worse" and "Zits."

I'm making plans to go to Chilliwack, B.C., in August to celebrate my 90th with the other granddaughters. I was there last year for my 89th and they want me back. Can you believe it? Me and my mouth?

Two new great-grandchildren are being welcomed soon and they must meet great-grandmother before she leaves this old planet. And who knows how soon that will be. Getting cremated so I won't have to keep looking good. Casket is a cardboard box (burns faster). I just can't figure out these people that have to decompose in a $12,000 mahogany job with those thousands of dollars worth of flowers. I prefer to smell any that come my way now while I'm alive. No need to wait until I'm dead to send flowers.

Your grandfather asked for his ashes to be sprinkled in the marsh where he did his duck shooting, and some in the bay at Port Rowan where he commercially fished for years. Right now they are residing in my clothes closet, waiting for a good windy day.

As for my ashes, I request that on another good windy day, you all stand down around the same marsh and let them fly. Actually, I could care less.

Have I told you what a wonderful job your sister Julie did singing at Grandpa's funeral? She and your Uncle Brad enter-tained the crowd of 230.

Sun is still shining today and I have just enjoyed a great nap. Cannot say I feel refreshed yet. I'm still a bit groggy.

Your mom stopped by the other evening and we had a good chat, neither of us ever at a loss for words.

Will get this in the basket for "outgoing" mail when I go down for my next meal. Social hour is at 5 p.m. and it's 4:35 p.m. now. A pile of walkers, all parked in the halls, lead to the dining room. I have been reduced to walking with a cane as I had three great falls, which always messes up my face. I even had a black eye. But you should have seen the other guy!

I'm reasonably happy in this place. The dining room is quite ritzy. Cloth napkins! I will never be able to use those flimsy paper deals again. The food isn't bad, and people are friendly and helpful. How can I ask for more?

Hugs and Love,
Grandma

Mary from Massey, Ontario, was also one of my frequent responders. She lived in the back woods, the polar opposite to my life in hustle-bustle Paris.

May, Canada

Dear Janice,

Thanks for your delightful letter! Not only did it arrive in time for Mother's Day, but also in time to share with the women in my knitting group. We take over the comfy chairs in the reading area of the local public library one afternoon a month.

I, too, walk, but not in city parks with statues and pugs, but along a gravel road in Northern Ontario. We live in the bush between the small communities of Espanola and Massey—an hour's drive west of Sudbury.

My walks take me along a trail through the bush where things are in the early stages of greening. I am fascinated with the minutiae of life—the pussy willows, the mosses, and the first violets. The road winds past fields bordered by bush and a creek that passes under (and sometimes over) the road.

I pick up the inevitable trash as I cannot bear to have this engaging, growing landscape be marred. As we age, my husband and I find ourselves more in awe of this piece of his paternal grandfather's farm we chose as our home.

Thanks for sharing the beauty of your chosen home. I am already looking forward to next month's letter.

Mary

June, Canada

Dear Janice,

Your letter about rain and bookstores brought much welcomed rain to Northern Ontario—forest fires, you know. No bookstores closer than an hour's drive so we rely on the public library for our day-to-day reading and its twice-a-year used book sales to stock up.

My son, Bruce, the one who lives in Simcoe and ordered your letters for me, has been following your blog and was telling me about your touring around. I had my sister and sister-in-law from Ottawa here for the first time ever, so I have been seeing my own neighborhood through someone else's eyes. I took them to Manitoulin Island one day to tour around, hence this card. Aside from the landscape—very different from around here—and the lovely non-chain shops, they were thrilled with cormorants and Sandhill cranes that they had never seen. They had to hop out of the car to take pictures of a pair of Canadian geese with twelve goslings that crossed the road in front of us and slid down the bank and into the creek that the road followed. None of this was new to me, but I was gobsmacked by the thousands of yellow lady slippers growing in the ditches. I thought we had been looking at dandelions until I had to slow down to make a turn and realized what they were. I had never seen yellow ones and in such profusion! There are four deep pink—almost burgundy—ones on my walking trail that thrill me, but these thousands took my breath away. I guess we just have to be open to the wonders around us.

I absolutely love the watercolor sketches that accompany your wonderful letters. Thank you for the personal note (on a piece of a Fitzgerald book!). What a clever, inventive woman you are!

Happy reading and exploring.

Mary

⌒

September, Canada

Dear Janice,

Glad to hear you are back in Paris. Hope the Canadian holiday lived up to the Euro boyfriend's expectations.

This card is from a restaurant I've been to three times this summer. It has a lovely garden setting and wonderful food. I have the same thing each time. I can't get past the Stilton cheesecake with salad greens!

The roadsides here are resplendent with the golds (goldenrod and tansy) and purples (asters of all shades of purple) and white

(Queen Anne's lace) to rest the eyes. The maples are beginning to turn and the ferns are browning. The Canadian geese and Sandhill cranes are gathering in the local farmer's fields. We are starting to hear flocks of geese go over at dusk and daylight. We suspect they overnight on our beaver pond, but the trail is steep and tricky, so night is not a good time to go see if they are there.

We spent the weekend with a group of friends in the South River, south of North Bay down Hwy. 11. I was there to learn to rug hook. Actually, now that I know how it's supposed to be done, I learned it's not going to ever be something I do. But good to get away and learn something new. We also had a couple of lovely dinners out and enjoyed the beautiful old house we rented.

I am busy dealing with garden produce before the frost gets the last of everything. Tomatoes and beans yesterday. Pears today.

I always look forward to your letters. Thanks.

Mary

In October, I received a letter from Mary full of what appeared to be amber-colored crumbs.

October, Canada

Dear Janice,

Fall here has also been "changeable." One day warm and lovely, the next gray and miserable. We actually had wet flurries today! I picked these leaves last month when they were at their peak and ironed them between sheets of waxed paper so hopefully they will stay intact until they get to you. The rain and winds have stripped most of the trees around here. Thankfully the evergreens fill in the spaces, even though they, too, have dropped lots of needles this year. Thanks for the soup recipe. Just happens I have some squash—three humongous ones from the garden. I have cooked one down and used it in muffins, pie, and "pumpkin" butter—a first try this year. It's definitely soup weather so I look forward to giving yours a try.

Off to a quilt show in Sudbury tomorrow with friends and taking part in a Fiber Festival next weekend. I am demonstrating the making and using of yo-yos—not the wooden kind—fabric circles gathered to look sort of like flowers. I am working on a pair of heavy wool/nylon blend work socks for our youngest son. Part of his Christmas present.

À bientôt!
Mary

Dear Áine,

Winter in Paris is light on tourists, heavy on rain, and very light on light. The place is plunged in darkness from late afternoon until 8 a.m. If I stay inside until 5 p.m., I'm out of luck for any chance of soaking up natural Vitamin D from the occasional ray of light. I've spent most of my time cozy inside with my sweater, blanket, and tea.

Dear Áine,

Winter in Paris is light on tourists, heavy on rain, and very light on light. The place is plunged in darkness from late afternoon until 8 a.m. If I stay inside until 5 p.m., I'm out of luck for any chance of soaking up natural Vitamin D from the occasional ray of light. I've spent most of my time cozy inside with my sweater, blanket, and tea.

The flower shops are selling hyacinth bulbs. I've brought a few of them home and watched them slowly burst forth in Easter pinks and purples on my window sill. It's more entertaining than looking beyond the windows to more gray—perpetual dusk.

The cafés are bustling par usual, except most patrons are inside, shoulder to shoulder, sipping their café crèmes. Only the smokers brave the seats outside, huddled together—puffing and sipping but never lingering.

For two days, it snowed enough for an army of small snowmen to appear. But then came the rain and all that remains are a few twigs and carrots. The wind has been particularly harsh, and when it arrives with the rain, they gang up, snatching umbrellas like common thieves and sending them crashing and rolling down the street until they slink and hobble like injured spiders.

Tonight there will be no rain, just cold. It may be a good night for cassoulet at the bistro up the street. Cassoulet is a bean and meat stew, and really, a fancy name for what we call pork and beans in Canada.

And tomorrow, another day of gray, followed by darkness, with the lamps working overtime to make the city look like a big birthday cake.

Janice

29

Potatoes and Proposal

I was burning a pot of potatoes on the stove. Smoke billowed and I started yelling about how dinner was completely RUINED and I spewed a lot of other choice words that Christophe would never find in his French-English dictionary. I really let those potatoes know just how I felt about how unkind they were to ruin dinner. Christophe stood by and stared. "Is this who you are?"

A question. An exhale. The truth. The truth is that this is not who I am. The truth is I was stressed about more paperwork from the French government requiring more information I didn't have and didn't know how to get. I was projecting my frustrations onto the potatoes. It wasn't their fault. I didn't know how to explain any of this to Christophe, so I sighed and shook my head. "No, this is not who I am."

He handed me a baguette. "We eat without potatoes. No problem." And it was done. Later that night in bed, he turned to me and whispered, "Darling, no more potatoes for you. It's my job now. I am Polish man. Potatoes no problem."

A few days later, the burning continued. This time, in the shower. The stupid shower of squalor. First, the shower curtain would slick up my leg. So gross. Even when I bought a new one, fresh out of the package, I felt like I was at the Bates Motel. To avoid the shower curtain, I had to lean back toward the tap that sometimes dripped hot water on my bum, which it did that day. I had reached my limit with this shower. I stormed out, wrapped myself in a towel, and stood dripping and heaving in front of Christophe who was happily strumming away on the guitar. "I...need...a new shower door...and new...taps." I was crying now. "My bum is burnt...AGAIN!" Now I was wailing. I had mentioned the shower door and taps before but was clearly not convincing. He began with his same reason as before, "It's not my house." And yes, a shower door did slide into the home renovation category, which would require approval or permission or something that always made him hesitate. But this time I had ammo.

My eyes narrowed. "I want a new shower door for my birthday."

Now, Christophe's greatest concern was gift-giving. He always freaked out, not knowing what to give and wanting me to be happy. So he was usually relieved when I told him exactly what I wanted. Here in this moment, I told him exactly what I wanted. He looked at me, dripping and shivering before him. He exhaled. "Anything for you, my darling."

A new shower door may not seem like a romantic gift, but after getting down to my one-suitcase life, I discovered that for me, lasting happiness comes from experiences, not things. And though a shower door is a *thing*, it would provide daily spa *experiences*.

After a few weeks of searching for a store that sells shower doors in Paris (not easy to find), we had it delivered, assembled it, and installed it in the bathroom.

And then.

He was standing in the shower. I was standing outside the shower. No one was touching the shower door that decided to, on its own accord, come crashing to the ground and break into thousands of tiny light blue glass pieces.

Here's something I learned that day about Christophe: when he was very mad, he *whistled*. I suggested warming up leftovers for dinner. He suggested going out for a beer afterward. We agreed. He shoveled up the glass and I got busy with dinner, both of us on opposite edges of the apartment stewing in our own misery. I wanted that shower door. He wanted to give it to me.

Soon he came out with a bloody finger. "Darling, I need something." I looked at his finger and grabbed for the bandage.

He went back into the bathroom, and I went back to the kitchen. He came back to the kitchen, got on one knee, and revealed an aquamarine ring, the exact shade of his eyes…and the exact shade of the thousands of pieces of glass scattered in the bathroom. The same ring I had picked out six months before and mourned over when it disappeared from the jeweler's window.

Oh my, I thought. Life is happening.

Christophe began. "I love you, darling. Will you stay my…" He didn't know the word for wife.

"Wife?" I said.

"Yes! Will you stay my wife?"

I didn't get into the verb correction between "to stay" and "to be." Later. Later. "Yes! *Oui!*"

Ring on, dinner ready, wound dressed. A perfect proposal. It was hardly a lobster dinner at the Rainbow Room, but it would do. He said later that he was probably going to propose on December 21 with an End-of-One-World-Beginning-of-Another theme, or possibly on Christmas. Or maybe after a nice dinner out. But on this night, he realized that this bad feeling about the stupid shower door had to be changed into a good feeling about something else. This is one of the many reasons why saying yes to him was easy.

Yes, yes, yes, and *oui!*

Two weeks later, another shower door arrived and this time it was installed without shattering. Good-bye, Bates Motel. Hello spa.

Dear Áine,

The City of Lights lives up to its name at Christmas. With the sun setting in late afternoon and twinkle lights draped from the trees, Paris is truly enchanting. There is something marvelous about walking briskly under the deep blue sky beneath the gaze of old street lamps, then popping into a boutique to absorb the cozy warmth. Parisians overheat their stores. Not that I'm complaining. I love it. Though I spend a lot of time peeling off layers.

The windows at the large department stores are a magical display of animatronic hypnotic wonder that keeps kids, young and old, gawking from the sidewalk. Usually a heavy hitter designer such as Karl Lagerfeld designs the windows to ensure they are très chic. Actually, the twinkle light displays are très chic, too. My street, rue Mouffetard, has a massive string of lights cascading down the street like a shimmery waterfall. It's all rather tasteful around here, which makes me wonder why many of the Christmas trees are heavily sprayed with fake snow of fushia, teal and — I am sorry to say — yellow. Where I come from you steer clear of all yellow snow. There isn't much snow in Paris, which is surprising since every tchotchke shop has walls of dreamy snow globes featuring the world's most recognized monument. That reminds me of a conversation I had with my old French teacher from my life before cafés and croissants. He had asked me if I'd ever been to Paris. "No," I responded. "I dream of Paris." He shook his head. "Mademoiselle MacLeod. You've got your verbs wrong again. It's not 'to dream,' its aller, 'to go.'"

Joyeux Noël!

Janice

Dear Áine,

The City of Lights lives up to its name at Christmas. With the sun setting in late afternoon and twinkle lights draped from the trees, Paris is truly enchanting. There is something marvelous about walking briskly under the deep blue sky beneath the gaze of old street lamps, then popping into a boutique to absorb the cozy warmth. Parisians overheat their stores. Not that I'm complaining. I love it. Though I spend a lot of time peeling off layers.

The windows at the large department stores are a magical display of animatronic hypnotic wonder that keeps kids, young and old, gawking from the sidewalk. Usually a heavy hitter designer such as Karl Lagerfeld designs the windows to ensure they are très chic. *Actually, the twinkle light displays are* très chic *too. My street, rue Mouffetard, has a massive string of lights cascading down the street like a shimmering waterfall. It's all rather tasteful around here, which makes me wonder why many of the Christmas trees are heavily sprayed with fake snow of fuchsia, teal, and—I'm sorry to say—yellow. Where I come from, you steer clear of all yellow snow. There isn't much snow in Paris, which is surprising since every tchotchke shop has walls of dreamy snow globes featuring the world's most recognized monument. That reminds me of a conversation I had with my old French teacher from my life before cafés and croissants. He had asked me if I'd ever been to Paris. "No," I responded. "I dream of Paris." He shook his head. "Mademoiselle MacLeod, you've got your verbs wrong again. It's not 'to dream'; it's aller, 'to go.'"*

Joyeux Noël!
Janice

❧ 30 ❧

A Baffled Bride

The moment the temperature dropped below trench coat weather, all the ladies of Paris started strutting their stuff in fur. I saw bulbous fur collars, puffy ear warmers, and fur coats that draped nearly to the ground. The whole city was a catwalk, and every lady was a supermodel.

I come from a world of animal rights activists, so all this fur made me gasp and wonder if they got the memo. The memo likely came around the same time as the memo about smoking being bad for health. The French likely rolled up the memos with tobacco and smoked them, declaring *"Joie de vivre!"* between puffs.

One blustery afternoon, I walked into a vintage clothing store. There were so many fur coats it was like being in a bear cave. I stroked a few that were so soft I wanted to name them Fluffy or Cuddles. Soon I was hugging them and leaning into the racks, whispering, *"Joie de vivre."* Weren't the French the most marvelous people on the planet?

November, Canada

Dear Janice,

Furs in November? Really? How cold is it there? I'm still just

putting a sweater under my fall jacket. Some days I just need a
T-shirt under my jacket! Though I do think you should definitely
indulge in a vintage fur. Chances are the fur is Canadian, bought
at the annual fur auction in North Bay, Ontario. Buyers come
from all over the world. You'd just be supporting the Canadian
economy and honoring your roots.

À bientôt!
Mary

Though the French were generally marvelous people, they
were insane when it came to paperwork. I started to suspect
they were nutty with red tape when I started watching home
renovation shows. In all these shows, the owner of the house
required a massive bookshelf to hold massive volumes of *binders*.
Binders made me shudder.

Now that Christophe and I were betrothed, we had to go to
City Hall to see what papers were required to make it happen.
We sat across from the lady in charge of such things. She pulled
out a large folder for us to take with us. Inside the folder were
forms to fill out and a very long checklist of other documents
to gather.

I mentioned to her that this was a lot of paperwork.

She said that marriage was much more thorough than just
getting a visa.

I thought back to my boobie episode at the visa office. How
much more thorough would getting married have to be?

Christophe and I started in earnest to gather our papers. First
on the list was an official copy of our birth certificates, translated by an official translator. Fine. We had the birth certificates
already. They just needed to be translated. Check! Photocopies
of our passports? Easy.

Then we had to get piles of forms from our embassies. Off
we went. We walked out of each embassy not with papers but

with appointments to return a month later to ask for the papers, which would arrive a month or so after that. All of these documents required translation, too, which required more appointments and more time.

Spring became a flurry of paperwork. Luckily, I had Mary from Ontario to remind me that the season was happening at all.

May, Canada

Dear Janice,

Spring has finally arrived here in the north after two weeks of summer heat and snow on Mother's Day. Now we have sunny, spring-jacket days with nights that are staying above zero.

It's lovely to walk and see all the different shades of green. We were remarking on how red the new maple leaves are in contrast to the rest of the bush. Today's delight was a large patch of yellow marsh marigolds. I saw bear, raccoon, and deer tracks in the mud on today's walk.

We are anxious to get seedlings into the garden, but know from experience it's still too early this far north. My husband has his greenhouse planted and we are hungrily watching the plants in his "salad bar" planter.

Bruce has guaranteed his continued inclusion on the Christmas list with this renewal. All the "second-hand" readers of these letters are thrilled, as am I.

Many thanks,
Mary

By May, six months after our first visit, we were able to return to City Hall with our bursting folder of papers. The lady went through them all with her lips pursed, hovering over each form with a red pen like a stern teacher. The official copy of our birth certificates had to be issued within six months and ours were expired. Off we went again to order new copies of the copies, which were to be translated by a translator again. The old translations wouldn't work. They had to be redone and stamped with an official stamp of an official translator. I couldn't help but wonder if this was a make-work project just to keep the eighteen city halls of Paris busy.

When we returned to the City Hall with our new papers, she informed us that there were other issues with other papers. *She couldn't have mentioned this before?* Off we went again for another few weeks. By the time everything was approved, she said we had to get married within two months or half the other documents we had gathered would expire. I thought of my gay friends who had recently won the right to get married in France. They didn't even know what they were getting themselves into. Poor lads. But Christophe and I were fine with getting married within two months. We didn't want to start gathering paperwork all over again.

After our complicated *dossier* of papers was approved, we started telling people the date of the wedding. All the French gave us congratulations, but not for the wedding. They congratulated us on getting our papers approved. The man at the post office summed it up nicely. *"L'administration est coo-coo!"* Complete with hand gestures.

As I made decisions about the wedding, I realized just how baffled a bride I could be. I was asked to provide the photos of what kind of wedding paraphernalia I liked: bouquets, wedding cakes, cake toppers, invitations, meal options, party favor preferences. I was clueless. What kind of bachelorette party would I prefer? Would I like a wedding shower too? It started to dawn on me that other girls had thick wedding *dossiers* bursting with wedding photos and decisions already made years before the engagement ring was ever purchased… or in some cases, before the man was even met! So I relied on

Pinterest and people who cared deeply about wedding details to make decisions for me.

I wanted a small, simple wedding. How quickly it mushroomed into three ceremonies: one legal wedding in Paris with a handful of friends and the Polish family; one religious wedding outside of Calgary on a lake with the friends (we had planned the vacation before the wedding date); and we would have one large wedding reception with my family in Ontario.

My mother and sisters planned the Ontario wedding, with my artistic sister Carla creating the invitations for all three. No small feat! My friends in Calgary planned the religious wedding, and I planned the Paris wedding, but really Melanie did most of the planning, which suited me just fine. She was my translator when visiting the florist and the restaurant, but she was also the decider. "You don't want that. Believe me. I've seen it. Looks terrible. You want this." I would nod, grateful for her advice and good taste. Maureen, Alison, and Shannon were the fashionistas. For dresses for wedding-related events (you mean there are events that I need dresses for too?) they sent me to the Karen Millen boutique at 6 rue des Francs-Bourgeois. I walked into the store and explained that I was a bride and would need fancy dresses for wedding-related events.

The word *bride* turns regular saleswomen into giggling, gleeful teenagers. They zipped around like kids in a candy store, grabbing dresses left and right, pulling out all the dresses that fit my description. Many options I pulled from the racks were no-gos. The lead saleswoman would do this finger wag and say, "Not for your body, but we try."

She led me to the change room and waited outside for me like a good girlfriend. Almost everything fit except for the dresses I had picked myself. See, they had sized me up the moment I walked into the store and knew exactly what would look best on my figure. They weren't trying to sell me everything. They were fitting me. That's the difference with the French. These aren't some girls who have a summer job in a clothes shop. These are women who work in the fashion industry in Paris. There is a difference. And they weren't trying to make me look younger or thinner. For the French, there is no problem to solve, only a chance to make something more beautiful, to bring out its essence. My saleswomen were *enhancing*.

"*Je suis professionnel!*" my saleswoman boasted when I complimented her on her choices.

I walked out of the store with three dresses that were me, but better.

Friends had warned me that the French were unkind. But if you let them be, meaning if you let them do their thing and trust that they take national pride in making everything more beautiful, you'll end up being more beautiful yourself. The reason you see so many beautiful French women of all ages is because they have teamed up through various divisions of labor to make everything and everyone a little more beautiful—from top to toe.

For my hair, I would go to Sylvie Coudray. Her *atelier* was just down the street from Chanel's first Paris shop on the famed rue Saint-Honoré, in the same apartment where Maximilien de Robespierre lived during his reign of terror after the French Revolution. In fact, she cut hair in his bedroom. I can just imagine him waking up and deciding whose head to chop first. And centuries later, Sylvie doing the same, but with hair and not heads. Sylvie is a tall, strong, blond woman. I liked her immediately. The first time I went to see her, she sat me down at a chair in front of a mirror and took me through a one-hour consultation before she even picked up her scissors. She explained that there was only one perfect hairstyle for me and she was going to give it to me. She pulled my hair up, pulled it back, moved it here and there to illustrate how other hairstyles wouldn't frame my face as well as this one haircut. "Why do most stylists concentrate on the back of the head when they should concentrate on the front? I don't understand this," she would say, shaking her head. She had big opinions about hairstyles that go through fads. "The worst was the Jennifer Aniston hair!" She rolled her eyes. "It looked good because it framed her face nicely. HER FACE. It wouldn't do the same for others, and yet women of the world insisted on it." She shuddered. "That was a dark time in my career." She started snipping away at my mane and proceeded to give me the best haircut of my life. It was me, but better. It was so lovely that I became instantly miffed by every hairstylist I've ever had. They just didn't know what they were doing! Sylvie understood. "No thought put into what would actually look good!" She took a breath and dropped her arms in fatigue. "Don't people know how to imagine what is beautiful and what is not?" I wasn't going to trust anyone else with my wedding day hair. Sylvie was a true artist.

I would need a wedding gown too. After cleaning out my closets back in Los Angeles, which seemed like another lifetime by now, and after seeing my friends shopping, I had low self-esteem with shopping. Melanie and Alison would walk down racks of clothes like two prongs of a divining rod, senses perked, searching and gathering, searching and gathering. I would follow, walking down the middle, looking calm on the outside, but inside I was a bubbling volcano of overwhelm. I didn't know where to start. I was picky and couldn't make decisions. I couldn't even pick out Christmas tree ornaments. And now I would have to pick out a wedding dress?

While I lamented to my mother about the prospect of having to buy a wedding dress in French in France, she said one thing: go to Belgium. Now this may not seem like sound advice to the average onlooker, but going to Belgium was going to solve all my angst about the dress. See, my cousins have a wedding dress shop in West Flanders, in a city called Roeselare. I would try on dresses in English in Belgium with help from my cousins. Knowing it was family, I was walking out of the joint with a gown for my big day. This was happening. One decision made.

I took a train. Four in fact. After all my traveling throughout Europe, getting to a small city in Belgium proved the most challenging of all. I arrived in Lille and had to buy train tickets for the local lines. Generally, in major ports, the signs all offer the local language and English, but here I only had French and Flemish as choices at the ticket booth. I was actually grateful to be able to communicate in French. Progress! But once fully in Flanders, I had a few stressful moments at some podunk outpost train platform in WhoKnowsWhere when I had four minutes to transfer trains. Finally, I ended up in Roeselare where my cousin was waving and running to greet me.

We got busy. I was in town for twenty-four hours and I would need to find a dress, get it altered, and leave the next day with it in hand. My cousin Véronique was fantastic. She whipped out everything in my size. I said yes, no, or maybe. All the yeses and maybes were set aside. In the big change room, standing in my delicates, I stepped in and out of many dresses, whittling the pile down to two lovely gowns. She was a pro. She knew what looked good and what didn't look good. She was not putting me in anything that didn't flatter my figure. When we made the final decision, the seamstress arrived to pin it in all the right places then took it away to sew, and we went out for a tour around town.

The next day, I hopped back on the train with my dress in hand. Adding the time limit helped me make decisions. Progress!

My bachelorette party, or a hen party as my English expat friends called it, became a cock and hen party as I invited Simon as well. We sat around a long table at our favorite wine bar, 5 Cru at 5 rue du Cardinal-Lemoine, and sipped wine as one by one they prepared me for marriage.

Alison advised me to enjoy everything. The good, obviously, but there are lessons in the bad and joy to be had there too.

The bad helps you set your course and informs you of what you don't want so you can veer toward what you do want. Melanie advised us to drink more wine. The maître d' and owner of the wine bar agreed and brought over another bottle. Simon advised me to be myself, to not try to change. Sometimes we can get flustered and fall out of line with our true desires. If I ever felt myself getting flustered, I should stand back, observe the moment, and center myself. There is wisdom there that can help me deal with a situation. Julie said that I must go to Vienna and attend a ball in my wedding gown. I didn't even know this was what people did. I added it to my list. Shannon's advice was to prioritize each other. When her grandfather came home from work, her grandmother would make him a drink and they would sit alone in the salon, away from the seven children who knew to stay away during this sacred *apéro*. Carole sat with her arms crossed and said that she had no clue what made a good marriage. "Good luck," she concluded. But then it dawned on her. "Maybe that's what it takes to have a good marriage. Good luck." Glasses were raised with wishes for good luck.

Tipsy and happy, I made my way home at the end of the evening armed with my list of wisdom from my friends. I was no longer baffled. I was ready to get married.

Dear Fine,

May 1st is Labour Day here in France. This means that those that have jobs don't have to work and those that don't have jobs attend demonstrations to scream about it. May 1st is also the day when you can buy small bouquets of Lily of the Valley from the street vendors dotted all over the city. The idea is to give the flowers to friends, but I didn't know about that until later, so my little bouquet is adorning my window and honoring my friendship to myself. My windows are finally open, and I can feel a warm breeze. Since winter lingered in Paris, the city was slow to turn on the fountains. For months, they were dry and silent, crusted with last year's fallen leaves. But now they are gurgling, spitting and splashing, in with wishes and centièmes. I'm not sure how the city manages the urban décor, but I'd like to think that a big meeting is called at City Hall – the who's who of Paris gather and agree that NOW would be the ideal moment to turn on the waterworks. The mayor nods and saunters over to a giant switch on the wall. Everyone holds their breath as he turns it on. Cheers, applause, and champagne follow. Meanwhile, water rushes through the labyrinth of underground pipes, along the metro tunnels and catacombs to reach the hundreds of thirsty fountains that explode in joyful rapture. And there I am waiting with a wish in my heart and a centième in my hand.

Amitiés (Best Wishes),

Janice

Dear Áine,

May 1st is Labor Day here in France. This means that those who have jobs don't have to work and those who don't have jobs attend demonstrations to scream about it. May 1st is also the day when you can buy small bouquets of lily of the valley from the street vendors dotted all over the city. The idea is to give the flowers to friends, but I didn't know about that until later, so my little bouquet is adorning my window and honoring my friendship with myself. My windows are finally open, and I can feel a warm breeze. Since winter lingered in Paris, the city was slow to turn on the fountains. For months, they were dry and silent, crusted with last year's fallen leaves. But now they are gurgling, spitting, and splashing, inviting wishes and centièmes. I'm not sure how the city manages the urban décor, but I'd like to think that a big meeting is called at City Hall. The who's who of Paris gather and agree that NOW would be the ideal moment to turn on the waterworks. The mayor nods and saunters over to a giant switch on the wall. Everyone holds their breath as he turns it on. Cheers, applause, and champagne follow. Meanwhile, water rushes through the labyrinth of underground pipes, along the Métro tunnels and catacombs, to reach the hundreds of thirsty fountains that explode in joyful rapture. And there I am, waiting with a wish in my heart and a centième in my hand.

Amitiés (Best wishes),
Janice

31

A Wedding in Paris... and Beyond

In the days leading up to the wedding, Christophe mentioned that I was running out of time to change my mind. I joked, replying that he shouldn't do anything that would make me change my mind. I added that I probably shouldn't do anything to change his either. He, in his infinite kindness, said that I could do anything and he would never change his mind. "Who loves who more?" His arms crossed. Chest out. Grinning.

The only time I had doubts about marriage was back when the lady from the city hall was taking her sweet time approving the *dossier*, akin to a big folder of the Vacation Request Forms of my past. Would she ever let us get married? But I never had doubts with Christophe. It would be my great pleasure to marry this man. *In Paris!* I still couldn't believe it.

Making it official was important to Christophe. Yes, it was important for him to show me how much he loved me by committing to me, but I also sensed he was starting to feel like he had family again. He'd gone twenty years floating without much more than a few phone calls at Christmas and the occasional visit to Poland. He shyly asked me one night if he could call my mother his mother, explaining with his manly reasoning that this is tradition in Poland. Tradition or not, my mom would be pleased to add him to the pack. He breathed easier. The worry lines in his forehead decreased.

He seemed to get younger as the wedding day approached. Young and happy.

For my wedding day hair, Sylvie snipped my bangs here and there, pinned in a dainty and sparkly tiara, and curled my hair into long relaxed tendrils. It was me, only much better. She, my sister, and my mother worked together to get me into my wedding dress. An elegant A-line floor-length gown, fitted at the bodice with halter straps wrapped around the back of the neck and a simple belt with a few sparkles. I looked and felt like a princess.

Christophe arrived to fetch the team. In some cultures, it's bad luck to see the bride before the ceremony, but in Paris, where there is no aisle to walk down at city hall, the bride and groom walk in together and leave together. A nice metaphor for life. *We're in this together. Two by two.* I thought he would wear his nice gray suit, but he walked in with a black tuxedo. Seeing him took my breath away. He looked even more like James Bond in his suit. "A black tuxedo?" I said.

He swallowed hard when he saw me in my gown. "I couldn't wear my gray suit," he said. "I am picking up a princess. I need to look like a prince, not a chauffeur." He took my hand and kissed the back. "Let's go, my princess."

The ceremony was at the city hall in the 5e arrondissement. This wasn't by choice. It is law that you get married in the city hall in your district. Every arrondissement has its town hall and mayor. I suspect this is for an easy division of labor for the thirty-five-hour workweek. You get married by the mayor or his deputy or you don't get married at all. There are no exceptions. But we were delighted to be getting married at city hall. Ours was a spectacular space with gold gilded walls and chandeliers that drooped with large, sparkly crystals. It was an iconic landmark, right between the Pantheon where France's biggest thinkers have their final resting place, and the Jardin du Luxembourg, the park that is my preferred resting place during my urban hikes.

Our group of fifteen gathered outside the great hall and we walked into the marriage room. The mayor arrived, with a red, white, and blue sash across his chest, looked at my last name on the register, and asked, "Highlander?"

I nodded. Even here. Even now.

He continued. "*Immortelle?*"

"*On va voir.*" We will see.

We had Team Poland, Team Canada, and Team France in attendance. Together, our united nations crew sat through twenty minutes of legal proceedings that had been set by the government since Napoleonic times. Each spouse owed each other respect, support, and assistance. "*Oui.*" We were both responsible for the material and moral guidance of the family and were to provide for the education of the children and prepare for their future. "*Oui.*" Each spouse was to contribute to the marriage expenses in proportion to their respective means. "*Oui.*" We were to protect our children in their security, health, and morality, ensuring education and allowing their development, showing regard to them as people. We were to make the children a party to judgments relating to them according to their age and degree of maturity. "*Oui.*" And finally, after these super romantic vows, we were both asked if we would take the other to marry. "*Oui!*" When we were to exchange the rings, they provided a silver saucer and gave a gesture to simply "go ahead." No big blessing of the rings. No "with this ring I thee wed." I suppose the French fought long and hard for a separation of church and state. We shrugged, and Christophe picked up my ring and put it on my finger. I did the same with his. A big kiss followed, flower petals were flung, and a marriage license was handed over in a blue velvet folder. Later, I opened the marriage license and noticed that my birthday was wrong. *Le sigh.* After all the birth certificates and copies of my passport I provided, it seems I would have to return to city hall later to correct an administrative error. But, for now, champagne.

Our group walked together to Jardin du Luxembourg for photos. Someone popped a cork, and glasses were filled. Rounds of cheers and laughter followed. After the photos in the garden, the group meandered down rue Mouffetard, and Christophe shook hands along the way with colleagues and shopkeepers who came out of their stores to see the wedding procession. When we arrived at the restaurant, our local Tourn'Bride at 104 rue Mouffetard, I threw my bouquet. It went soaring high and well over the ladies with arms stretched and landed with a thud behind them. Oops. My sister fetched it, and I offered it to Carole, wishing her good luck with a wink.

One of the men pulled out a chair and sat it in the middle of the street. I sat and Christophe slowly removed my garter, invoking sniggers and jests from invitees and onlookers. He sent it spinning into the air where his nephew caught it. (A few weeks later he would ask his girlfriend to marry him and she would gleefully accept.) We laughed and walked into the restaurant for dinner. It was there when Milena, the youngest of Christophe's family from Poland, stood to say a speech. She was a doe-eyed, quiet brunette, still learning English. And though she was merely fifteen, she spoke like a true matriarch. She spoke of how Christophe's mother wished to see him married and taken care of like her other two sons, but she knew she would die too soon. His mother always wore a gold necklace with a leaf pendant. Upon her death, the family decided that Christophe's wife would have this necklace and they tucked it away for twenty years until this day in Paris where her only granddaughter would present this necklace to me.

There wasn't a dry eye in the house.

I was so proud of this young woman in this moment, and instantly so aware of how important it was for the women in this family to keep traditions alive. After all my letting go of the material, along came this young girl to remind me that some things are worth keeping. That some mementos mattered.

Milena was strong, assured, and sweet as she struggled to say all this in English through her tears. And now, I had more than a necklace. I had someone to look to for times when I will be charged with tasks of a matriarchal nature. Eventually, it would be up to us.

Later that night, I changed out of my wedding dress and into a white sundress (one of the wedding-related event dresses from Karen Millen). A few of us took a riverboat down the Seine to the Eiffel Tower and watched the light show. *Quelle romantique*!

In the wee hours of the next morning, we hopped a plane to Toronto, another to Calgary, and yet another to the lake in the mountains. We spent a glorious week sitting on the porch and barbecuing with friends. Why did we have our honeymoon with a group? Because the trip was planned well before the wedding was even considered. And as Christophe pointed out, our whole life is a honeymoon. "The matching robes!" One morning, as the waves lapped quietly against the shore, we decided that it would be a good day to do it all again. I pulled out my wedding dress, he pulled out his tux, and we gathered for our own ceremony at the edge of the lake, this time with seven friends. My friend Mary conducted the ceremony and was also the maid of honor. She had scrounged up the readings from her wedding, which suited us just fine. One person recited a reading from the Dalai Lama, another recited a Native wedding blessing, another did the Our Father. Christophe recited his vows in Polish, and I recited mine in English. We pulled off our rings and set them on a silver saucer similar to the one in Paris. But this time all of us hovered our hands over the rings and gave them a blessing, serving of a visual reminder of this day when our love was sealed.

With this ring, I thee wed.

Wind rustled in the trees. The train from across the river tooted its horn. We kissed.

Tanned and relaxed, a week later we flew to Ontario to do it all a third time. We had the reception at the golf course where my brother-in-law Brian was the greens keeper. While my sisters and mother were planning the event, he said that he'd try to keep the grass green by the clubhouse. And my other brother-in-law, Otto, helped deliver and assemble a massive wedding cake my sister Carla made for the event. This was a true family affair.

This was the first time Christophe had seen just how large my immediate family was, a whopping ninety-four invitees. "It's wonderful," he said. "A dream. And now it is my family, too. *Merci, merci encore.*" After I spoke to the crowd, thanking everyone for this and that, he said a few words. He turned to me and said that before, he didn't believe in God, but then one day an angel sat down at a café and he believed. For a man of few words, he certainly knew what to say and when to say it.

I always thought I would get married in Canada and honeymoon in Paris. Not the other way around.

Our rings were from Poland, my dress from Belgium, and the marriage license from France. It was an international wedding, rather fitting for a Polish French boy marrying a Canadian California girl.

32

How to Be an Artist

After that day at the Vatican three years before when I went to confession, I finally got glad about all the dreams that hadn't come true. I didn't have a boyfriend. I didn't have kids. I didn't have a mortgage. I had nothing holding me down in California, which was the groundwork that made it possible for me to leave and find a life more suited for me in Paris. That priest was right. If I didn't have it, I didn't need it. I finally got glad about that instead of just wondering why I didn't have it yet. It would come in time. But back then, it was just me thinking of my dreams and scribbling them down in my journal.

I became kinder to myself too. I let myself stay home and paint rather than go out "just in case my soul mate was there." I started enjoying the process of unraveling my apartment and of not having as many choices in my closet. I walked more. I bought myself flowers. I started this journey by getting rid of clothes, but eventually I slowly peeled off the layers of judgments I had placed upon myself for failing to get married by the ripe old age of thirty-four. For failing to find happiness in my chosen career. For creating a life that wasn't much fun. I let myself off the hook. I forgave myself for the judgments. The truth is that I did the best I could with what I knew at the time. And at some point, I had the good sense to change my usual self-inflicting, unnecessary, and lame New Year's resolution from an uncreative "lose ten pounds" to a simple practice of writing in my journal. It was this slight change that got the ball rolling.

Doing yoga, murmuring through a rosary, meditating, going for walks, and yes, writing in a journal—these were all outward actions of the same thing. They were daily practices that slowed me down enough to help me unwind a life that wasn't working and start building a life that did. For me, the journal worked best. For others, talking it out in therapy could work best, or even just shutting up. Silence is a great way to hear our inner wisdom. I didn't realize when I started my grand journal-writing experiment that I had all the answers inside me. Sometimes my inner wisdom took on the form of Mr. Miyagi, Percy Kelly, or Ernest Hemingway. I would ask a question of them in my journal and let the pen roll. I didn't care if I was making it up or channeling. Either way, it was a way to access my inner wisdom, and it was always soothing and insightful.

When I was twenty, I was living in Toronto and loving my new career as a copywriter. I was in a bookstore leafing through greeting cards. One card stood out from the rest. It was a small card with one sentence written on the front. The card is long gone now. Perhaps I used it to write a letter to Áine. But I never forgot what the card said on the front:

Write to learn what you know.

And what did I need to know? First and most obviously was that I had all the inner resources I needed to effectively deal with my situations. And secondly, I needed to realize that I was an artist. Not the one who paints letters about Paris. The artist who is the head honcho creative director of her own life.

We must know how to design our lives. We are all artists, and each day is a canvas. Writing in my journal each day was how I redesigned my life. I became conscious of just how much I disliked my day-to-day existence. I would get up, react, and repeat. I had created a fast, busy, messy life. There was no one else to blame. I designed it, tried it, didn't like it, and had to erase and redesign. But I didn't know I had to erase and redesign until I carved out a container of time to write each day. Finding the time was challenging. Sometimes I stole time during office hours to write. Sometimes I lied to friends, saying I was busy, so I could stay home and write. I did whatever I had to do to be with my practice. At first I felt guilty about this, but eventually I began to make it a priority. I insisted on it, even at the expense of a few billable hours or hurt feelings of friends.

That journey led me to Paris and into the arms of the lovely Christophe. I started to see Paris differently. No longer with the bright enthusiasm of a tourist, nor was I blind to it as a longtime resident. I started to see Paris as a canvas. A blank wall near a fountain became a place where I could write a letter. The cobblestones of a street would meld to become words on the page. The lapping waves of the Seine turned into words written with a drippy fountain pen.

After my morning coffees with Christophe, I walked around the city with my camera, capturing scenes that I would take home with me to paint on days when the clouds were too gray, the pavement was too wet, or the wind was too strong. As I painted, I imagined the letter I would write, describing this time of my life in Paris. I deliberately omitted certain unpleasantries. There was no room in my letters for the vulgarities spewed by mad men belching on the street, the army of thieves who literally rob the city of its charms, or the constant and abrasive loudness of tourists.

The longer I painted, the more I realized so much of my life had been in training for this moment in time. The most obvious training was the painting classes I took sporadically along the way and the career as a copywriter that taught me to write. But also the weekend workshop in bookbinding I took a few years ago that taught me how to fold hundreds of papers neatly and quickly came in handy when folding my hundreds of letters. Less obvious training was the stock market that pulled my investments down low enough to rev me up to create a money-making project in Paris. And it was easy with my Etsy store that was already open, the PayPal account that was already set, and the fans from my blog that were already there waiting for me to tour them around Europe via painted letters. All these bits of training melded into a collage that unleashed the artist in me. When looking back, this training was so perfectly arranged that I couldn't help but think there was someone wiser than myself pulling the strings.

Whenever one of my painted letters was dry and ready to copy, I walked it carefully over to the print shop. The print master greeted me with his usual "*Bonjour*, MacLeod of the clan MacLeod."

"*Bonjour*, Norman," I would reply. He was French, though his name was not.

Norman would smile at my latest work of art and make the copies. I would walk the box of letters home and address each one. Dear Matthew, Dear Heather, Dear Kelsey…and I meant it. Dear lovely person. You are dear.

I have sent over ten thousand painted letters about life in Paris so far. The original plan was to afford daily life and keep pushing my buffer of money further ahead of me so I had plenty left for when I retire. Suze Orman would be so proud. But now I'm building up funds for the next adventure too, making sure I keep my wardrobe down to one suitcase. Well, with Christophe, two suitcases.

After my wedding gown was stored and the final thank-you card mailed, I took to running and walking through Jardin des Plantes, around the corner from the mosque that serves the most delicious mint tea. In the park, there are two long, tree-lined lanes that have been pruned inward, creating a shaded verdant canopy. Each morning, I walked or ran with a tissue in one hand (allergies!) and my keychain with all my keys in the other. One day, for no reason at all, my house keys fell off the chain and landed on the ground. Just my house keys. This seemed physically impossible. And yet, there they were in the sand. I picked them up, refastened them to my keychain, and continued on my run. Upon returning home, I checked the mail. Another beautiful letter from Mary describing the joys of life in the country.

When Christophe came home from lunch, I told him about the keys. "But how?" he asked. I shrugged. Over a lunch of brie, baguette, sliced meat, and salted tomatoes, I translated Mary's letter. He sighed. After his time in Canada, he wanted to move there, to a house on a lake. A place where we could have children and a garden and grow roots. For him, Canada was the perfect present, but for me, it was my imperfect past. I was still haunted by high school bullies who I feared running into at the grocery store. I explained this to Christophe.

"That is all done now, my darling," he said.

I looked at the keys and Mary's letter. I nodded, understanding that I could choose to see Canada as he did, in the present with the fresh eyes of a tourist, and that there was an expiration date on my childhood that was met long ago. Perhaps I could evolve the Paris Letters to write Garden Letters. I could make it work. I would figure it out, with Christophe at one side and my handy journal at the other. I nodded.

He took my hand and kissed the back. "Let's go, my princess."

BONNE ANNÉE

Dear Áine,

Happy New Year! In Paris, they say "Bonne Année," and often answer with a singsong "et Bonne Santé" – and good health. Back home, we wish each other a prosperous New Year, but in France, prosperity isn't as big of a mark of success. In fact, the French have been known to chop off the heads of anyone who has risen above the crowd. All this probably explains why, when the world is talking about fiscal cliffs and recessions, the mayor of Paris is talking about carousels. Paris has recently added 20 more carousels to the 35 permanent ones in its collection as a gift to citizens and visitors of Paris.

Now, along with being the City of Lights, it's the City of Carousels. And the rides are FREE! All winter, these merry-go-rounds of wonder sparkle like whirly jewels. Don't think for one minute I won't be trying to out-race kids to get to the best horse. Game on! I've been living in Paris for a while now. I thought the enchantment would fade, but then the carousels came to town and I'm back to being amazed, my mouth agape in awe around nearly every bend in this magical city.

Warmly, Janice

Dear Áine,

Happy New Year! In Paris, they say Bonne Année *and often answer with a singsong* "et Bonne Santé" —*and good health. Back home, we wish each other a prosperous New Year, but in France, prosperity isn't as big of a mark of success. In fact, the French have been known to chop off the heads of anyone who has risen above the crowd. All this probably explains why, when the world is talking about fiscal cliffs and recessions, the mayor of Paris is talking about carousels. Paris has recently added 20 more carousels to the 35 permanent ones in its collection as a gift to citizens and visitors of Paris.*

Now, along with being the City of Lights, it's the City of Carousels. And the rides are FREE! All winter, these merry-go-rounds of wonder sparkle like whirling jewels. Don't think for one minute I won't be trying to out-race kids to get to the best horse. Game on! I've been living in Paris for a while now. I thought the enchantment would fade, but then the carousels came to town and I'm back to being amazed, my mouth agape in awe around nearly every bend in this magical city.

Warmly,
Janice

January, Canada

Dear Janice,

Loved the carousel painting—And to think the rides are free! Here is one old lady who would be pushing not only the kids, but you sweet young thing out of the way, too!

Bonne Année et Bonne Santé seems a very appropriate wish for around here as there is much malaise going around. For the past two years, I have been snowshoeing with a couple of women. Our first real snow came the week before Christmas and I have been out faithfully tromping my trails ever since. Now that they are usable and well-packed, one friend has sciatica and the other has been battling the flu since before Christmas—ergh! So I am tromping alone.

I chose this chickadee card as we have a small flock that we feed all winter. They get quite friendly and quite cheeky if the food isn't put out on time!

We saw the flying squirrels the other night (on the feeder), the first since last spring. We have a feeder at one of our windows, easy to just open and put out the food, and gives us a great viewing spot. Last night there was a fat, furry raccoon cleaning off everything the birds had left. I thought he'd have been sleeping by now, but maybe it hasn't been cold enough to really put him out.

You've been in Paris over a year! I'm so glad to have been part of the first discoveries and enjoyments. I think if one really loves the place where they are, there are always enchantments to be found. Keep looking.

Mary

33

Paris Letters

One of my subscribers is the copywriter who took over my old job. Each night after work, he walks up to his front door and pulls out mail from the box. Most of it is the junk mail that he created during the day. He checks a few headlines, then tosses most of it in the recycle box. But then, inside the stack, he spies a little letter from Paris. A grin forms. He takes the letter into the house, sits on the couch, and exhales the tension of the day. He opens the letter and begins to read.

Dear Jine,
I've got the
Fitzgeralds on my
mind these days.
F. Scott & Zelda — the
emblem expats of the 1920's
Lost Generation in Paris. It was
in these cafés, on cold wintery days,
where they sat huddled together writing,
sipping and discussing their work. "What do you think
of The Great Gatsby as a title?" he would ask, and history would
be made. Right here in these cafés! It boggles the mind. Eventually,
madness and jealousy came along, but before they did, F. Scott & Zelda sat in these
cafés kissing, writing each other love notes, piecing together storylines and poems,
always believing the happiness would never end and inspiration would seep
out of the sidewalk. These days, I sit in the same cafés and wonder if I'm
sitting next to the future F. Scott or Zelda. Perhaps they wonder the same about me.
What do you think of Paris Letters as a title?   Au revoir! Janice

February 2013,
Paris

Dear Áine,

I've got the Fitzgeralds on my mind these days. F. Scott and Zelda—the emblem expats of the 1920s Lost Generation in Paris. It was in these cafés, on cold wintry days, where they sat huddled together writing, sipping, and discussing their work. "What do you think of The Great Gatsby as a title?" he would ask, and history would be made. Right here in these cafés! It boggles the mind. Eventually, madness and jealousy came along, but before they did, F. Scott and Zelda sat in these cafés kissing and writing, piecing together storylines and poems, always believing the happiness would never end and inspiration would always seep out of the sidewalk. These days, I sit in the same cafés and wonder if I'm sitting next to the future F. Scott or Zelda. Perhaps they wonder the same about me. What do you think of Paris Letters as a title?

Au revoir!
Janice

My Little and Big Acts to Save Up or Not Spend $100 a Day

1. Canceled my television service.
2. Sold my television. Saved money and time.
3. Used up my samples from Sephora.
4. Used up free things from swag bags given out at film industry events.
5. Used up all my cosmetics that were on the brink of their expiration dates.
6. Used up the creams that were just so-so before I repurchased my favorite.
7. Stopped buying things just because they were on sale and a good deal.
8. Stopped buying decorative items for my apartment.
9. Sold everything I didn't use on a daily basis on Craigslist and eBay.
10. Traded clothes and bric-a-brac at the thrift store for a tax receipt.
11. Paid off my credit cards, thereby not paying interest or late fees.
12. Sold a few paintings on Etsy.
13. Added small price tags to the finished paintings I hung in my house. Visitors often bought without me feeling like I was selling.

14. Donated paintings to charity auctions instead of buying at the auctions.

15. Gave paintings as gifts, thereby not buying gifts.

16. Stopped buying art supplies and used up what I had.

17. Sold all the art supplies I had left.

18. Stopped going to energy-zapping group dinners.

19. Stopped spending time with draining friends (usually by not joining them for dinner).

20. Invited friends out for hikes, coffees, or frozen yogurt rather than wait until they invited me to pricey dinners.

21. Lied to friends. Or more specifically, told some of them I was busy when they invited me out. I think angels purposely put people in our path to ask us out to do fun things the moment we decide to take time for ourselves. It's as if they are asking, "Are you sure?" Yes, angels! I'm sure. Stop giving me free tickets to see Dave Matthews!

22. Accepted free tickets to Dave Matthews. C'mon. It's Dave Matthews.

23. Used up my running shoes. I had enough with enough zip to get me through the year.

24. Oatmeal.

25. Gave away books on my blog.

26. Scanned in photos and important documents then sold my scanner.

27. Became vegan, which is cheaper than eating meat. However I also became anemic, so I should have added iron supplements.

28. Drank all the tea in my house before buying more. Oh lordy, I had a lot of tea.

29. Drank all the protein shakes in my house before buying more. Same.

30. Took all the vitamins I'd bought. Same.

31. Went out on picnics and used up the plastic forks, knives, and chopsticks I had saved over time.

32. Traded stocks.

33. Actively participated in my health care plan. I got check-ups galore before I hit the road to make sure I was healthy. Preventative care, yo.

34. Stopped having house parties. They drained my soul and pocketbook.

35. Got my taxes up-to-date. Refund. Score.

36. Had car-free weekends. I took my bike instead and saved on the gas.

37. Near the end, I sold my car.

38. Sold my bicycle too.

39. Ordered a small coffee instead of a latte. It would have been cheaper to make coffee at home, but less social.

40. Said no to dinners at restaurants.

41. Stayed home at night and painted instead.

42. Took myself on reading dates instead of real dates.

43. Gave up on dating. There was always something to buy and I wasn't interested in a romance once I had my eye on the road.

44. Stopped with the heavy (and therefore pricey) extra scoop of macaroni and cheese at the Whole Foods salad bar.

45. Also stopped with the mashed potatoes.

46. Stopped going to salad bars and started chopping my own vegetables.

47. Cooked at home. Startlingly easy if I planned ahead.

48. Only went to movies I actually wanted to see. In LA, it's easy to get in the habit of going to every movie just to be fully educated.

49. Used up my movie gift certificates.

50. Did my own nails with all the polish I already bought.

51. Accepted gifts from people. Strange, but the more I released, the more I received gifts, largely in the form of free meals and stationery. I received them with a grateful thank-you.

52. Played guitar at night instead of watching TV. I did not sell my guitar.

53. Welcomed overnight guests into my home. Strange, but they basically fed me half the time out of gratitude for the free place to stay, and I was delighted to see them.

54. Traded my big seventeen-inch MacBook Pro and bought a smaller MacBook Pro. There are cheaper computers out there, but no. No, no. No.

55. Got a cheaper phone plan.

56. Got a cheaper phone. Most of those gigabytes were wasted on me anyway.

57. Searched my medicine cabinet before I went to the pharmacy. What I needed was usually in there.

58. Cancelled my online dating service as I had given up that my love lived in LA.

59. Stopped taking birth control. Saved the cash, but really, I wasn't getting much anyway.

60. Listened to language CDs from the library.

61. Stopped walking into used bookstores. The temptation was too great.

62. Stopped falling for coupons. You know what's cheaper? Not buying it at all.

63. Sold all my furniture except my couch that no one wanted. Ben ended up taking it off my hands, thereby saving me the Apartment Clearing Fee that I would have had to pay to my rental agency.

64. Sold my refrigerator to my rental agency. I figured the new renters would need a fridge. My friend Emily suggested this idea. I made them an offer and they took it.

65. Discussed the best way to sell things with my friends. They often knew.

66. Sold my kitchen table and used the cash to buy a coat from Patagonia, which I still wear nearly every day in rainy Paris.

67. Never EVER stopped having a housekeeper. She was cheaper than therapy.
68. Stopped going to therapy. It all worked out.
69. Tap water, not bottled water. It all worked out too.
70. Water, not wine.
71. Cheap wine...it's a process.
72. Posted a donate button on my blog. Some people even donated.
73. Sent them thank-you cards from the stashes I found in my art supplies.
74. Stopped believing in storage solutions. The solution is to clean out closets.
75. Wrote lists in my journal nearly each day about what I could do to save up and pare down. I didn't finish these lists each day but I flipped back eventually to cross everything off.
76. What I didn't cross off wasn't important anyway, and because of this, I crossed it off.
77. Hiking, not shopping.
78. Cleaned out closets like I was looking for loot. Sometimes I found some.
79. Imagined the possibility of being able to save up enough to quit my job.
80. Took the investment advice from rich old men at my coffee shop.
81. Took care of unfinished business instead of ignoring it and going shopping instead.
82. Started acting like an adult with my finances.
83. Wrote about my plan on my blog so I felt accountable to someone.
84. Went to the beach often.
85. Declined invitations for weekends away. I figured I'd have plenty of weekend getaways in my future life.
86. Declined a few out-of-state weddings of people I wasn't

really close to. Sending them a more generous cash gift was more cost-effective financially and energetically.

87. Went to the gym at lunch instead of to the mall.
88. Eventually canceled my gym membership.
89. Hosted meditation classes at my house. The leader gave me the class free.
90. Spent all my coins. The bigger your coin jar, the bigger your coin collection.
91. Cashed in all my free coffees from loyalty cards.
92. Made plans to visit gardens around the city with friends. Walk and talk is *gratuit*.
93. Listened to all the music I already had in my collection. There was so much I didn't know I already had.
94. Stayed close to home on weekends, thereby saving on gas.
95. Switched from having house parties to going to TV-viewing parties at other people's houses.
96. Popcorn popped on the stove.
97. Used up all the half-filled journals I already had around my house.
98. Babysat my godson. I didn't get paid but it kept me from going to the mall. Plus it was fun.
99. Convinced my family to not get each other big Christmas gifts. Instead we got each other a small stocking stuffer. It was delightful, and no one missed the lack of presents.
100. Prayed that this nutty plan would work.

Thank You

M any thanks go to my blog readers, especially to Jeff Gelberg, Melissa Maris, and Bethoney Imbeault who have read and commented on nearly every single blog entry since Day 1. To Bruce Springsteen for writing the opening lines of *Thunder Road*. It was the spark that made me a writer.

To Laura Yorke, my literary agent, who instinctively knows where to be strong where I am weak.

To the team at Sourcebooks. Your support not only makes better books, but better authors. To my editor Shana Drehs who helped me rearrange mountains of text and tell a better, more cohesive story. And thank you also to sharp-eyed editors Anna Klenke and Sabrina Baskey-East.

To Melanie Brown who is my little focus group and gives me her honest opinion on each Paris Letter. To the rest of my team in Paris: Alison Abbott, Carole Le Roux, Simon Gallagher, Julie Legg, and Shannon Hindmarch. To my team in Rome: Claudio Dentale, Marco Giancarli, and Sandro Pierantoni. To my team in Canada: Patricia and Allan Markin and the entire FitzGerald clan in Calgary, Scott Cornfoot, Áine Magennis, and especially Karen VanOoteghem and Rob Sale for introducing me to the works of Percy Kelly. And to my California Team: Ron and Mary Hulnick and the University of Santa Monica, Sharon Yamamoto, James Lee Stern, and the infinitely talented musician and advice giver Paul Freeman. To my team in Poland: Jarek, Jola, Łukasz, Conrad, and Milena Lik.

And to my mom, Agnes MacLeod, for always reminding me that I can come home. You are my roots. To my dad, Bob MacLeod, for pinning up maps all over the house. You are my wings. To my sisters Julie and Carla for the small acts of kindness and extra loads you carry beyond always fetching me at airports.

To my grandmother, Betty Brown, for your lovely letters. You made me laugh.

To Mary Caldwell, for your lovely letters. You made me dream.

To all the subscribers of my painted letters from Paris. Infinite thanks for your kind words and support.

And to the lovely Krzysztof Lik. *Je t'aime. Kocham Cię.* I love you. You are my sunshine.

About the Author

J anice MacLeod is an artist. She is the creator of the Paris Letters. This is her third book. She is married to the lovely Krzysztof Lik. They live in Paris...for now.

PHOTO CREDIT: DAVID BACHER